AGAPE

AGAPE
LOVE CARRIED MY CROSS
PASSION IN ACTION

Crushing Curses, Healing Hearts, Saving Souls

By Nanette Crapo

XULON PRESS ELITE

Xulon Press
2301 Lucien Way #415
Maitland, FL 32751
407.339.4217
www.xulonpress.com

© 2020 by Nanette Crapo

All rights reserved solely by the author. The author guarantees all contents are original and do not infringe upon the legal rights of any other person or work. No part of this book may be reproduced in any form without the permission of the author. The views expressed in this book are not necessarily those of the publisher.

Unless otherwise indicated, Scripture quotations taken from the King James Version (KJV)–*public domain.*
Red Letter Edition, King James Version. Translated out of the original tongues and with the former translations diligently compared and revised. Authorized King James Version. The World Publishing Company. Cleveland and New York. Published by the World Publishing Company 2231 West 110th Street Cleveland 2 – Ohio

Scripture quotations taken from the New King James Version (NKJV). Copyright © 1982 by Thomas Nelson, Inc. Used by permission. All rights reserved.

Scripture quotations taken from the Holy Bible, New International Version (NIV). Copyright © 1973, 1978, 1984, 2011 by Biblica, Inc.™. Used by permission. All rights reserved.

Printed in the United States of America

Paperback ISBN-13: 978-1-6322-1278-8
Hard Cover ISBN-13: 978-1-6322-1279-5
Ebook ISBN-13: 978-1-6322-1280-1

Special Dedication

○ ○ ○

"The only thing that counts is faith expressing itself through love." <u>Galatians 5:6</u> (NIV)

This special dedication is to my mother, **Mary Foust Crapo**. She was the epitome of agape to and for everyone she met. Every friend she ever made became a lifelong friend that she would do anything for, and they would do anything for her. She stayed in communication through cards, letters, visits and the occasional expensive long-distance phone calls. She would have thrived on the many multimedia platforms of communication of this day and age.

The church was packed at her funeral with friends and relatives even though she had moved to another state some thirty years prior. Momma expressed her agape (love) through her actions, deeds and kind words. In doing so, she expressed her faith in Jesus through her love for others.

She is still missed and loved by all that knew her. Momma's legacy is her agape for Jesus which she shared with everyone she met through the light in her green eyes and the sincerity of her beautiful smile.

I love you, Momma. You live on in my heart and I know I will see you again when Jesus comes to take me home!

Thank you, Jesus for blessing me with the fruit of the Spirit of Your agape kind of love. Thank you for blessing me with my mother's heart of compassion!

Nanette Crapo

Today is 02/12/2020, the 38th anniversary of her passing from this world to be with Jesus.

Dedication

This book is dedicated to everyone who has ever suffered depression, to whatever degree and from whatever cause. Unfortunately, I believe that covers just about everyone. GOD spared me from such trauma as sexual abuse as a child, drug and alcohol addiction, and physical abuse. I cannot begin to understand what you have suffered; but I can testify as to the scars of emotional and psychological abuse. There is no doubt in my mind that GOD spared me the trauma of sexual abuse as an innocent child because He knew I would have been completely and irreversibly broken spiritually, emotionally and mentally. There is no doubt in my mind that I would have spent my life in a mental institution in a catatonic state! As it was, I so very nearly ended my life due to the emotional and psychological abuse of repeatedly being betrayed and rejected by those that were supposed to love and protect me.

That you are still standing is proof that GOD has made you strong where I am weak, and that He has a plan for your life. My heart goes out to you for your suffering. The fact that I am still standing is proof that GOD has made me strong with a loving, giving and forgiving heart where others are weak because they do not know the love of Jesus. My heart goes out to those suffering souls as well.

No matter what the circumstances or what the atrocities against you may have been, we have all been exploited by the devil. That's right! The real enemy is the devil and the only Superhero in this book is Jesus. He loves you, He knows what you are going through, and He weeps for your pain. Jesus is closer than you think. Draw near to Him and hold on with all the strength you have left! Only Jesus can crush your curses, heal your heart and save your soul. Only Jesus can and fill you with peace, love and joy. *Trust in Jesus Christ as your Savior; He is the only way to Father* GOD.

Nanette Crapo 03/08/2019

Table Of Contents

∘ ∘ ∘

PREFACE XI
SPECIAL DEDICATION V
DEDICATION VII
INTRODUCTION XV

I.   SECTION 1 CRUSHING CURSES 1
    A. CHAPTER 1 LIES OF SATAN 3
        1. "You're Fogotten" 5
        2. "You're Not Appreciated" 6
        3. "You're To Blame" 7
        4. "You're Rejected" 8
        5. "You're A Burden" 8
        6. "You're Invisible" 9
        7. "You're Not Worthy Of Love" 10
    B. CHAPTER 2 DISOBEDIENCE 13
    C. CHAPTER 3 DO-IT-YOURSELFER OVER-ACHIEVER ... 19
    D. CHAPTER 4 IDOLATRY 27

II. SECTION 2 SURRENDERING "OLD MAN" SELF 33
    A. CHAPTER 1 DOWNWARD SPIRAL 35
    B. CHAPTER 2 END OF SELF 47
    C. CHAPTER 3 DAMASCUS MOMENT WITH JESUS 55

III. SECTION 3 ASK SEEK BELIEVE FIND TRUST 65
    A. CHAPTER 1 **ASK** THE LION OF JUDA 67
    B. CHAPTER 2 **SEEK** THE SHEPHERD'S VOICE 77
    C. CHAPTER 3 **BELIEVE** THE PROMISES OF GOD 85
    D. CHAPTER 4 **FIND** THE LAMB OF GOD 93

- E. CHAPTER 5 TRUST THE FINISHED WORKS OF CHRIST 101

IV. SECTION 4 HEALING HEARTS 107
- A. CHAPTER 1 JESUS KNOWS........................ 109
- B. CHAPTER 2 AGAPE THE LOVE LETTER APRIL 10, 2019 119
- C. CHAPTER 3 THE CROSS PASSION IN ACTION 127

V. SECTION 5 SAVING SOULS........................139
- A. CHAPTER 1 EKKLESIA CALLED BY MY SOUL'S MATE 141
- B. CHAPTER 2 ARMOR OF GOD...................... 149
- C. CHAPTER 3 MISSION OF AGAPE "FOLLOW ME" MARK 8:34 157

VI. PRAYER OF SALVATION 163
VII. EPILOGUE...165
VIII. THE LORDS PRAYER 167
IX. ADDENDUM 04/04/2020 COVID 19..................169
X. ACKNOWLEDGMENTS 171
XI. REFERENCES 175
XII. SPECIAL MENTION 176

Preface

God speaks to me in visions, dreams, thoughts, occurrences, miracles, and other people more and more often. The closer I draw near to Him, the more I hear Him with clarity. All the praise and all the glory for this book belongs to Father GOD, for without Him I would not have even made the attempt to write it, let alone to think of writing it. Without Jesus I would not have a testimony. Without Jesus I would be a lost soul. Without Jesus I would not exist.

My journey with Jesus while writing this book has been a season of healing for my heart and soul. Along the way I have discovered His will for me; His calling for the rest of my life. GOD has definitely called me to serve Jesus... *ekklesia*. Ekklesia is when one is called out or set apart as in a church or a gathering of people that come together to serve Jesus. "Baba ekklesia", I am an uneducated babe in the body of Christ, but I have been called out to serve Him.

It has been revealed to me that the Holy Spirit has given me the gift of healing. Not healing as in miraculous cures though I am not counting those out, for *if it be GOD's will then it will be*. No, since my retirement and time spent on this journey with Jesus in GOD's Word and while preparing for this book, GOD has revealed to me that:

> *I am to pray for those with wounded hearts and shattered souls; as these are subjects that I have first-hand knowledge about. Jesus has healed my own brokenness during the journey of this book and in turn I am to share Jesus' love story with other broken vessels through my testimony.*

This journey with Jesus is actually my autobiography which is interwoven with scriptures from GOD's Word, <u>The Holy Bible</u>, to me and through me by His Holy Spirit. He placed it in my heart to write my life's story as a journal of sorts. I am but the messenger, the messages are from GOD. GOD's anointing is not only upon this book as I write it; but upon my entire life. It is truly supernatural, without a doubt in my mind. It has been a journey of necessity to eradicate my ignorance with understanding in His Word in order to heal my brokenness and in doing so, the brokenness of you the reader. Each new day during the journey of this book, Jesus drew me nearer with His agape kind of love. The kind of love He expressed for you and me at the Cross.

You will see many scriptures in this book as I have provided them for you to keep you from interrupting your journey with Jesus to look them up. In November of 2018 it was placed into my heart to write a book. That was confirmed in January 2019 while watching television. The pastor on t.v. looked right at me and said that GOD told him to tell me to write my book. That got me off the fence of indecision! His words spurred me into action; so I started spending untold hours researching in <u>The Holy Bible</u>, GOD's Word, with His Holy Spirit to guide me.

It has been an intensive roller coaster ride of emotions. He has been educating me, destroying my ignorance, and lifting me up out of the self-made ruts around my self-made hellish mountain of despair. Those ruts were becoming my own personal "pit" of depression.

> That endless circular journey of emotional anguish and depression of being unable to climb that mountain through my own pitiful efforts was detaining me from my appointment with Jesus on the road to Damascus.

This journey is also one of love and betrayal that goes all the way back to Adam and Eve's disobedience to Father GOD. It is necessary to expose the Eve in me if eyes and ears are to be opened so that others may repent as I have. The curses upon Eve extend to all of humanity, men as well as women, because all are in danger of loving someone or something too much, which is love that belongs to GOD.

The most important and mind-blowing awakenings in my mind, heart and soul were revealed to me through this journey of understanding the Truth and Mysteries of the gospel of Jesus Christ:

- The Truth of why Jesus came as a vulnerable man, born of woman and allowed Himself to suffer death, hell, and the grave out of His limitless Passion for us.
- The mystery of how Jesus expressed the magnitude of His faith and agape kind of love for Father GOD, for you, and for me; and how that faith and love gave Him the strength to endure the burden of the Cross that He carried for us all.
- The truth of why the Cross was necessary and how the Holy Spirit quickens us into eternal life.
- These are just a few examples of the mysteries of the gospel of Jesus Christ, and still there are so many more to discover!

"Abba, Father GOD, why have you chosen me to write this book? I do not know enough of your Word to write a book; no one will read it..."
Nanette Crapo, January 2019

I asked that question before starting the first book. I had prayed in a state of complete and utter despair that He put the pieces of me back together again. GOD told me in my heart that it is because *my spirit is wounded, and He would heal me through our journey together as "we" write this book.* Much of this book was originally part of my first book titled **ANGELS SPIRITS AND A 9 MM SCREW, Legacy Of Faith And Love Through Five Generations**. Along the way I realized the original book was about two separate seasons of my life, so it became two separate books. That is how and why both books were written simultaneously.

It is my sincere prayer that you allow yourself to become submerged in His Word through this testimony. And I pray that you too will open your heart to Jesus, invite Him in and experience his agape love through a personal one-on-one relationship with Him. If you do, you will never again be lonely. You will be loved beyond what your mind can comprehend. Your heart will be saturated with His love to the point of overflowing.
Nanette Crapo 02/12/2020

> **"that Christ may dwell in your hearts through faith; that you, being rooted and grounded in love, may be able to comprehend with all the saints what is the width and length and depth and height —to know the love of Christ which passes knowledge; that you may be filled with all the fullness of God."**
> **_Ephesians 3:17-19_** (NKJV)

Introduction

✦ ✦ ✦

(Taken from Section 4, Chapter 2)

All of a sudden the following words came into my heart like a lightning bolt! They are from Jesus to my heart through His Holy Spirit that dwells within me! It is very clear to me that I am to share them with the world! I call His message, "*The Love Letter*". I pray that **they** *penetrate deep within your heart and sear your very soul as they have mine!*

'Really? Your Everything?

Why do you cry for those that can give you nothing of what you seek or need?
Why do you cry for love lost that was nothing but lies and trickery from the beginning?
Why do you cry for waiting so long for your true soul mate?
Why do you cry for your broken heart and shattered soul?

<u>*What do you know of such things*</u>*?*

Have you suffered the betrayal and rejection of thousands upon thousands and thousands more?
Have you stood faithfully outside the doorway of time itself, knocking; waiting patiently throughout eternity for hearts to open to you?

Have you suffered physically the torment and agony of being scourged, willingly taking the burden of the sins of the world upon your broken body; then willingly being crucified upon the Cross by the very ones whose sin debt you paid for with your own life's blood?

<u>What do you know of betrayal and rejection?</u>
<u>What do you know of a broken heart and a shattered soul</u>?

Is not My love enough for you?
Is not My heart enough for you?
Is not My shed blood, My life, enough for you?
How much more of everything do you need from Me before you stop crying for your lost love?

I Am He that stands before you daily...
I Am He that loves you unconditionally and for evermore...
There Is No Other!'

WOW!!! I am at my local library, typing as fast as these thoughts have come into my heart. I sit here crying for the Passion in His Words. I am at a loss for words right now...

> **"The LORD has chastened me severely, But He has not given me over unto death." <u>Psalm 118:18</u>** (NKJV)

I cannot read the above without crying with a mixture of shame for taking His love for granted and of glorious awe for the depth of His Passion that has saturated my heart! I never want to forget His Words to me, to us! They have been engraved upon my very soul! Jesus is Agape...pure breathtakingly blinding love the likes of which I have never experienced from another and never will! The love I craved from man is nothing compared to the love I now embrace from Jesus! His Love permeates my very soul! His love will not fade away from me; it will not betray me; it will not judge me; and it

will not be taken from me! His love is mine forever and my love is His forever! Forgive me Jesus, for being so blind! I love You Jesus!
Nanette Crapo, April 10, 2019

Jesus has chastised me with His profound love that what I have been seeking all my life is already mine. Jesus Christ is my Heart, my Love, my Soul, my Soul Mate, my Everything! All of a sudden the complaints that caused me such lifelong hopelessness that nearly grieved me to the point of suicide seems so petty and insignificant! And to think that I almost ended my life because of that lonely emptiness from being rejected and not feeling loved! At long last my heart is full, my soul is complete!

Heavenly Father knows all my sins and all the secrets of my heart for His Holy Spirit dwells therein. He knows the shame in my heart for taking the love of Jesus and all that He has done for me for granted. I truly do repent, and I know I am forgiven. I have been cleansed by the Redeeming Blood of Jesus Christ. Jesus truly is my Everything and I shall never forget that! My love for Him comes from deep within my very soul! I wish to proclaim to the whole world... "***I love You Jesus, with all that I am!***"

> *"Repent therefore and be converted, that your sins may be blotted out, so that times of refreshing may come from the presence of the Lord," Acts 3:19* (NKJV)

Section 1
Crushing Curses

◦ ◦ ◦

"...and her desire shall be for her husband and he shall be the ruler over her." **Genesis 3:16** (NIV)

❍ ❍ ❍

"When he lies, he speaks his native language, for he is a liar and the father of lies." <u>John 8:44</u> (NIV)

❍ ❍ ❍

Chapter 1
Lies Of Satan

○ ○ ○

This is my personal journey of growth from the darkness of ignorance, to the milk of babes, to the meat of His glorious Word in The HOLY BIBLE. I prayed in complete brokenness in November 2018 for Jesus to put the pieces of *me* back together again by His grace and mercy. It is He that gave me the Grandpa that instilled the trusting, unwavering faith into my innocent child's heart that Jesus loves me. Faith in that truth has remained with me and protected me throughout many years of danger and heartache. The Apostle Paul even wrote of the importance of faith in Ephesians regarding the armour of GOD, which you will be seeing more of later in this book.

> *"In addition to all this, take up the shield of faith, with which you can extinguish all the flaming arrows of the evil one." Ephesians 6:16 (NIV)*

I am not a theologian, nor do I claim to be. And I do not think of myself as an author for all the glory belongs to GOD. Everything written in this book has been born out of my personal experiences throughout this journey called life. It is for all practical purposes my autobiography but more importantly it is my testimony. GOD speaks to me, educates me, protects me, corrects me, and guides me through His Word and the Holy Spirit that dwells within me.

I have been on this walk with Jesus since I could walk! But I am finding out that I only knew the concept of Him. Since the day I heard about Jesus when I was 3 and ½ years of age I have known He loves me, and He is always with me. I have never doubted that He is real and that His Daddy is GOD. I have accepted His presence with me 24/7 with the faith and unconditional love of a child. However, I did now know Jesus on a personal level.

Deep within my soul I always knew there was a profound secret behind Jesus. Yes, I accepted Him as my LORD and Savior at age 15, but I knew there was more. And somehow I knew that my misfortunes in life were brought upon me by myself. I just did not know how or why. It was only when I began to ask, *"Why is this happening to me over and over again... what am I doing wrong?"*; instead of the self-pitying cries of *"Why me GOD?"* that He lead me to the answers. If I had grabbed hold of Jesus and sought to draw closer to His glorious Light, instead of being content to walk along in His protective shadow, my journey of discovery would not have taken forty years. Instead of just knowing and loving Him, I would have been enjoying a *personal one-on-one* relationship with my closest Friend, my LORD and Savior, Jesus Christ.

Discovering the who, what, when, where and why of my backsliding years has been full of life altering revelations. Not only did I discover who I strayed from; what the consequences for straying were; when and where I went astray and why (hint... believing lies of the devil); but also how Jesus brought me back from the edge of self-destruction. Careful! Don't be quick to lay this book down thinking it doesn't apply to you. You might be as surprised and as blown away as I was to discover yourself in this book on this journey with Jesus.

I found that I had many sins that were against the will of GOD! I did not know that what I was doing out of love for others were sins against GOD! And therein lies the problem, I did not know! That is a pitiful excuse born out of ignorance for lack of knowledge in GOD's Word. There really is no excuse... none whatsoever!

Yes, I know we all sin or we would not need Jesus as our Savior. However, although I was baptized in water and redeemed by the Blood of Jesus Christ at age 15, I was a backslider by the age of 23! So, where did I go wrong? That, my friends, is what this journey with Jesus is all about. It is not about a religion. Rather it is about building a personal relationship with Jesus Christ. You are welcome to come along. His arms can hold us all! This is my story; this is my testimony.

I pray the following stories explain how the seeds of low self-esteem were planted through lies into my vulnerable child's mind. These stories expose what the lies were, who introduced those lies, when and where the lies were introduced and how those lies lead me to backsliding in my adult years. They are not meant for excuses nor sympathy, rather they are meant for setting the cracked foundation of the why for my lifelong quest for love.

Why should you care? Because, the devil exploited GOD's gifts of the *fruit of the Spirit* (Galatians) of my character and used them against me for evil. No one escapes the devils evil deadly schemes because he is a predator. The following stories of my life are examples of how he exploited my compassionate heart at a tender age and planted seeds of low self-esteem, low self-worth and low self-image that led to loneliness, helplessness and hopelessness. Those seeds were planted into my mind and over the years they infected my heart and soul with a deadly virus from the devil... depression. I am only now understanding that these were all lies of the devil with one purpose in mind, to destroy my faith and love for Jesus Christ, my Savior!

(Disclaimer: this is my own personal description of my depression; not a medical characterization or diagnosis. If you think you may be depressed, seek professional help and seek Jesus!)

-1-
"You're Forgotten"

Once on a vacation pit stop, I was left behind in the bathroom because I was "too slow". Please let me add that my mother made me wait to be the last one to use the facilities because I was "slow and always the last one out", as she often stated. These were only words, but they planted seeds of low self-esteem in my young heart. I am certain that it was not my mother's intention to do so. Anyway, this was back in the days before travel centers with the multiple untold number of bathroom stalls. On our vacation trips there was only one toilet for women and one toilet for men at the gasoline stations along the way.

My sister, myself and my mother, along with my baby brother Max, would all have to take turns. My eldest brother, Darrell, was old enough to go to the men's restroom with my father. By the time it was my turn, which was last, everyone else was getting into the car. When I came out of the restroom I found myself alone. The car and everyone in it was gone! I was eight years old and terrified of having been forgotten and left behind so far from home! By the time I had rounded the corner of the building I was crying. There they were, waiting for me... laughing at the trick played on me. Looking back I suppose it was to teach me a lesson or to make me faster. But the lie from the devil was that I was forgotten and left behind. That thought was forever etched into my memory.

-2-
"You're Not Appreciated"

Occasionally, I would clean out the garage. Never did I hear, *"job well done."* It is obvious to me now that I truly was craving approval. That need for approval was never voiced by me nor did I ever hear words of approval. Instead, if a tool came up missing I was accused of throwing it away.

I could not understand as a child why my father would think that I would throw something away that was not even mine? This too would hurt me deeply. In all likelihood, he knew exactly where everything was in his disorganized mess and did not have time to look for it in the organized drawers. But I was too sensitive and believed in the lie the devil was planting in my defenseless mind that I was not appreciated. God did bless me with a very good memory, and I was always able to produce the "missing" item(s).

-3-
"You're To Blame"

One Easter my mother was ill and was not able to give us the traditional Easter with the dyed eggs and baskets full of goodies. We got up early that Easter morning full of excitement, but there was nothing there from the Easter bunny! My father took us kids outside to show us the *"bunny tracks"* in the dirt by the back door and said, "Nanette walked in her sleep" (something I did until I was about ten years old) "and she scared the Easter bunny off". Needless to say, my siblings were mad at me for a very, very long time. After all, candy only came around three times a year, four if you counted the tiny valentine hearts. They eventually forgot, I think, but I did not. My father said I scared the bunny away so even I believed it really happened for as long as I believed there was an Easter bunny! I was to blame, no one else… just me. More lies the devil implanted into my young impressionable brain which were stored into my memory forever.

I was a clumsy child, the proverbial *bull in a china closet*. So whenever something was found to be broken, I was the first to get blamed. If I was the first to speak in denial, I heard, *"the guilty dog barks first"* (???). On the other hand, if I said nothing at all, I heard how I *"looked guilt"*! (???) I never understood either saying nor where they came from. Anyway, this scar of being blamed for everybody's everything also affected me deeply. *Thinking about it now, Jesus knows ten times ten thousand how I felt because He carried the blame, suffering and shame for everyone's sins even though He was without sin!* Of course, I am not without sin and I do not compare myself to Jesus! It is just that as I reminisce I feel the pain of loneliness and rejection all over again. Suddenly I realize that what I felt was nothing compared to what Jesus must have felt! I realize as an adult how much my parents loved and nurtured me and my siblings! It was the devil's plan to make me feel singled out for blame which nurtured my feelings of self-pity and seclusion.

-4-
"You're Rejected"

My parents did not attend my baptism even though the church was only three blocks away from our house. In fact, I do not remember any kind of reaction or comment related to my baptism. It was as though nothing special was happening. For some reason unknown to me even to this day, religion and politics were never, and I stress *never*, discussed in our house.

On another occasion I overheard my mother telling one of her friends that I would not pass the State Board of Nursing examines because I never studied. Well I did pass, and it was never mentioned again. On the other hand, neither were the words *"job well done"*, or *"we knew you would do it"*, or *"congratulations"* ever spoken. Every effort I made to win their approval seemed to be in vain. My mother never knew that I overheard her make the previous statement, so she did not know the devil used her off handed remark to cut me to the quick. Here again, I know her remark was not intended to hurt me, but it was the intention of the devil to instill in my vulnerable young heart that I was rejected and unloved by those that mattered most to me in my life. Lies, lies and more lies!

-5-
"You're A Burden"

Once again, I overheard my mother (and once again, unknown to her)saying she hoped that I would elope as she did not want to have to deal with the wedding plans! That was the most hurtful thing I had ever heard her say; especially, as she had done absolutely everything for my sister's wedding three years prior. So, I planned my own wedding, made two of the bridesmaids dresses myself, and paid for everything out of my meager savings. I was 23 years old, fresh out of college and without a full-time job. Therefore, it was not the elaborate ceremony such as I had always dreamed about having as my budget was very limited.

I went shopping by myself for my wedding dress, flowers, cake, photographer, invitations, etc. A trip to the beauty shop was out of the question, so I did my own hair and makeup, but not my nails. My nails were just as they always were, not even with gloss. I did not have any jewelry except for my engagement ring. There was something old, a 1951 penny; something new, my wedding dress; something borrowed (I think it was the penny doing double duty); and something blue, the traditional blue garter.

I did not ask for assistance nor did I ask anyone to shop with me for my dress. I did not think anyone was interested, and I did not want to be a further burden. Thus I developed the habit of doing things by myself as an isolated loner. Just an added thought here... doing things by myself has kept me lonely and isolated even in marriage or in an auditorium full of people. That aloneness pushed me closer and closer toward the pit of depression. Believe me when I say that my mother would have been happy to help me if I had asked and she very likely was disappointed that I did not. However, my misconception was that she would say, *"No"*, so I never asked. In fact, I find it difficult even to this day to ask anyone for anything. It is a miracle that I have learned to ask GOD for all my needs, but I am getting ahead of myself.

-6-
"You're Invisible"

Even though the previous story happened about sixty years ago it still haunts me to this day. I admit that it still hurts my feelings in a *deep-seated emotional psychological scars of a middle child* sort of way. You know, the invisible one in the middle. It was as though I was not part of the family or that I did not even exist. I not only felt forgotten and rejected, I felt invisible. I unknowingly made myself invisible because of the lies of the devil. I hid out in my room to avoid being singled out and blamed. During my preteen and teen years my room was my sanctuary. My room was where I went to bury myself in the life found on the pages of LITTLE HOUSE ON THE PRARIE books by Laura

Ingalls Wilder. I would daydream of being loved by a family such as hers. Being alone was not what GOD intended for me, nor does He intend it for you.

Of course, as a child I did not know why I was lonely. I did not put 2 and 2 together that by removing myself from others I was causing my own loneliness. I did not know the devil was filling my thoughts with self-pity to lower my self-image and self-worth. I did not know at the time what GOD has to say on the matter; but I am learning!

-7-
"You're Not Worthy Of Love"

I do not remember hearing the words, *"I love you"*, and I do not remember receiving hugs or kisses from my parents. This is no exaggeration! I do not dwell upon it as it cannot be changed, but to dredge it up for this book brings back insecure feelings of unworthiness. The only hugs and kisses I ever received growing up were from Grandpa and Grandma Crapo. Need I tell you that I lived for those summer vacations? I never understood as a child why my parents could not hug me and tell me that I was loved. I truly believed that I was not worthy of being loved by my parents and later in life, by my husbands. Even in marriage I had to initiate the hugs, the kisses and the words, *"I love you"*.

As an adult I realize that my parents made every effort not to show favoritism. They did the best they could from what they learned from their parents. Their love was demonstrated by their protectiveness. They provided all our needs and loved us all equally and unconditionally. Jesus loves us equally and unconditionally too; no matter what! No one can out love Jesus!

> *"I have been crucified with Christ; it is no longer I who live, but Christ lives in me; and the life which I now live in the flesh I live by faith in the Son of GOD, Who loved me and gave Himself for me." <u>Galatians 2:20</u>* (NKJV)

I know some people have truly been rejected and unloved, not just through misperceptions such as myself, but in actuality. The pain of rejection and loneliness, for whatever cause or reason, is still devastating and lingers without an expiration date. My heart goes out to all of you. I pray this book helps heal your heart and soul as you journey along. Jesus can touch your heart and heal your brokenness as well as mine. His love is limitless!

I have not thought of any of these stories for many, many years. Apparently they traumatized me deeply or they would not be so painful to recall now. I suppressed them rather than to deal with them. Suppressing hurtful issues is what I learned to do during my stint in a psych ward (not as a nurse, but as a patient) with severe depression and an impending nervous breakdown.

The devil will plant seeds of doubt with every opportunity he can find. He is relentless! He had me in bondage to my low self-esteem. I was defenseless in my ignorance without the Word of GOD!

> *"Put on the full armour of GOD so that you can take your stand against the devil's schemes."*
> *Ephesians 6:11* (NIV)

◦ ◦ ◦

"Then the LORD God said to the woman, 'What is this you have done?' The woman said, 'The serpent deceived me, and I ate.'" <u>Genesis 3: 13</u> (NIV)

◦ ◦ ◦

Chapter 2
Disobedience

∘ ∘ ∘

"Let no man deceive you with vain words; for because of these things cometh the wrath of GOD upon the children of disobedience." Ephesians 5:6 (KJV)

Please take heed of GOD's Words and do not be tricked by the lies of the devil nor the slick words of the nonbeliever. Especially, whenever you find yourself on the rebound from the betrayal and loss of someone you trusted and loved. My young adulthood was the beginning of my backsliding in the pursuit of my heart's desire for a soul mate. Desire for my husband, Eve's desire, Eve's curse, became my own. At least that is the lie the devil had me believing. Lack of knowledge in GOD's Word made me vulnerable. I cannot stress that enough!

There are millions upon millions of the devil's puppets, knowingly and unknowingly doing his bidding to prey upon GOD's children (believers in Jesus Christ). Through my ignorance I was obedient to such people while thinking I was being good. Honestly, I thought in my heart that I was doing what GOD wanted me to do: *"love, honor and obey"* my husband. After all, those are the vows that I said before GOD in my marriage ceremonies. But in reality, I was being disobedient to GOD because of my unawareness of His Word.

"A persons steps are directed by the LORD. How then can anyone understand their own way?" Proverbs 20:24 (NIV)

Lack of knowledge was the catalyst to my disobedience. Disobedience, in turn, continued to accelerate my ignorance into foolish decisions until I became an *ignorant fool*. Jesus tried to open my eyes and turn me back to Him. I did not realize that Jesus was calling me back to the fold because I did not realize I had strayed. More importantly, I did not recognize His voice because I did not know His written Word. Reading my Bible would have given me a better understanding that the stories about the lives of those found within its pages are not fables, fairytales, legends or old wives tales. They are all about real people with real issues of life that still apply to us today. They are there for our education about life, the evil ways of the devil (he even tempted Jesus), and the many mysteries of Jesus Christ as well as His great love for us. I was sinning and I did not even know it! That is to my shame! I did not have a clue that the devil was manipulating the scriptures to lure me into disobedience.

"Woe unto him that striveth with his Maker!"
Isaiah 45:9 (KJV)

My woes were brought upon me by me, myself and I. The consequences of disobedience were upon me. The weight of carrying that burden in my heart was almost unbearable as I could not let go of the rejection and the loneliness. The devil had me wanting to just give up and end it all because, after forty years, I did not see anything changing anytime soon. That has been the devil's evil scheme from the beginning of time. He will do anything and everything to get me back to the depth of depression that I started with in the hopes of getting me to end my own life before fulfilling the plans GOD has for me. But I wised up after that first attempt and there will never be another. Praise GOD!

I would venture to say that almost everyone, especially us women, know the curse upon Eve for eating of the forbidden fruit of the tree of knowledge. She was cursed to have pain during childbirth. Even I knew that much. But how many of you readers know of the other two curses Eve brought upon herself and all womankind because she disobeyed GOD? I for one did not have a clue there were three curses. In addition to those three curses put upon women through Eve, we are all (men and women alike) under the curse of death through the disobedience of Adam! More knowledge of GOD's Word revealed during my research on this journey of healing.

"To the woman He said:
'I will greatly multiply your sorrow and your conception;
in pain you will bring forth children;
Your desire shall be for your husband,
And he shall rule over you."
<u>*Genesis 3:16*</u> (NKJV)

And your desire... and he shall rule... and, and. These were three separate and distinctly different curses put upon woman through Eve for her disobedience to GOD. *As* for the curses mentioned above, well, I am blown away! It explains my deep desire to please my husband for sure. It explains why I felt I was nothing without being married, as though I had no other purpose in life!

Satan twisted the curse of Eve's desire for her husband and utilized it against me by preying upon my low self-esteem and my need to be needed and loved. He chained me into bondage of desire for my husband and into bondage of addiction to the institution of marriage itself. Yes I was addicted to being married and to loving my husband. Both gave me a false sense of belonging and of being loved. I did willing submit myself to my husband allowing him to become the "ruler" over me which was the third curse upon Eve for her disobedience. Satan does not let a curse go to waste. I have been a naïve and helpless pawn in his evil schemes in my blind ignorance for most of my life! It is time to expose these lies. The enemy does not want me to tell you the truth that Jesus Christ freed us from those curses and from the laws of sin and death when He took our place upon the Cross!

> *"Christ has redeemed us from the curse of the law, having become a curse for us (for it is written, "Cursed is everyone who hangs on a tree.)"* <u>Galatians 3:13</u> (NKJV)

GOD's Word is beginning to open my spiritual eyes and ears. Jesus is providing the main bulk of the material through the supernatural guidance and teachings of His Holy Spirit as I read scriptures! As I read and learn with understanding of His Word, I am more and more able to plant seeds to His glory and spread the gospel of Jesus Christ.

I ask you to seek the truth for yourself. You may be able to prevent lies that have been planted by the devil from causing you to suffer the consequences of disobedience that may be even worse than mine! Or, if you are already suffering said consequences, the truth about Jesus can and will enlighten you and turn your circumstances around if you but seek Him. "How, you ask?"... read His Word and store them in your heart until you can tell others about them.

> *"Then the LORD put forth His hand, and touched my mouth, and the LORD said unto me, 'Behold I have put My Words in thy mouth.'"* <u>Jeremiah 1:9</u> (KJV)

Holy Spirit has awakened my heart and my mind. He has let me know that what I thought was love was but a misguided distraction of the devil to give away to others that which belongs to my only true heart's desire, Jesus.

Nanette Crapo April 2019

○ ○ ○

"and to make it your ambition to lead a quiet life: you should mind your own business and work with your hands, just as we told you." [1 Thessalonians 4:11](NIV)

○ ○ ○

CHAPTER 3

Do-It-Yourselfer Over-Achiever

∘ ∘ ∘

The devil had lured me off the narrow path of righteousness and onto the wide road of backsliding and the consequences thereof with each failure in life, each failed marriage, each failed relationship. Satan took GOD's Words out of context and manipulated them to suit his purposes. Then he reinforced his lies in my heart; the heart that GOD gave me as He formed me in my mother's womb.

> *"This is what the LORD says—- your Redeemer, who formed you in the womb: 'I am the LORD, the Maker of all things, who stretches out the heavens, who spreads out the earth by myself..."* <u>Isaiah 44:24</u> (NIV)

Each failure made me try harder. If I could just win their approval maybe they would like me just a little. In my pitiful state of desiring to be wanted and loved, being liked was a hopeful start. Desiring to be loved, or at least liked, has made me strive to be the best I can be. Thus, the do-it-yourselfer over-achiever was born.

In my world, everything has a place, and everything is in its place. OCD (Obsessive Compulsive Disorder)? I do not know as I have never been diagnosed as such. Whatever I do, I give it my all. If that effort is not good enough I keep after it until I am satisfied. If something is out of place I do not freak out or anything, I just quietly put it back where I think it belongs. After all, it does not matter to those around me. If my husband said "jump" I would said, "Sure baby! How high baby? If that's not high enough, I'll try again baby!" They had me jumping because it confirmed their control over my life and because they enjoyed watching me bending over backwards to please them! I know! I know! It makes me want to heave now! The truth hurts, but it is setting me free!

> **"Sanctify them by the truth; Your word is truth."
> John 17:17** (NIV)

Just because you cannot hear Jesus and you do not know He is talking to you does not make it untrue that He is! My problem was that I was too busy plotting and planning my self-made world, unable to hear Jesus screaming at me to get away from unrighteousness because I did not even know such unrighteousness existed! I was doing everything myself to prove my worthiness. I was laboring to earn love from those I loved; love that should have been given freely.

Bottom line is I had not been educated in GOD's ways. If I had I would not have been manipulated into following unrighteousness. I would not have knowingly been disobedient and gone against GOD's will. I would not have become a do-it-yourselfer, over-achiever backslider! I would not have been saying to GOD (through my self-reliance) that I did not need Him!

We all need help. GOD wants us to seek help from Him in prayer. His desire for us is to be dependent upon Him. In doing so, we are admitting that we can do nothing without Him and that we believe by faith He will fulfil the promises of His Word. Only this year am I learning the truth of how the enemy exploited my misinterpretations. He took GOD's Word and twisted it around to make it sound good. Out and out lies to make me rely upon what I *thought* I was supposed to do and not what GOD had planned for me!

> *"For my thoughts are not your thoughts, neither are your ways my ways, declares the LORD."* **Isaiah 55:8** (NIV)

I believe in GOD's promises. GOD's Word is His bond, His promise to us, and GOD cannot lie!

> *"For when GOD made promise to Abraham, because He could swear by no greater, He sware by Himself."*
> **Hebrews 6:13** (KJV)

> *"...in which it was impossible for GOD to lie..."*
> **Hebrews 6:18** (KJV)

Can you see how the path of unrighteousness gets wider, steeper and slipperier as one strays farther and farther off? I would never in a million years have thought of my mousey self as being prideful without having read it in His Word! Now that I know, I can see it clearly. I was very proud of being the one to fix everything. I was very proud of being faithful, of being self-reliant and of being a child of GOD. Oh, yes, so proud in my self-righteousness. I did not know about such things until I read it... how could I?

All the time I was chasing false dreams! It was the farthest thing from my mind to be disrespecting and second-guessing GOD! If only I had been armed with His Word, I would not have been so easily conned by the lies of the smooth-talking, silver-tongued serpent. I would not have succumbed to the one's that exploited my trustworthy nature, luring me into the ungodly pit with them. GOD's warnings are clear about such things. If only I had read my bible sooner... if only.

> *"But, dear friends, remember what the apostles of our LORD Jesus Christ foretold. They said to you, 'In the last times there will be scoffers who will follow their own ungodly desires.'* **Jude 8:17-18** (NIV)

> *These are the men who divide you, who follow mere natural instincts and do not have the Spirit".*
> **Jude 8:19** (NIV)

I truly believe that I missed the one that GOD had chosen for me. He had asked my father for my hand in marriage before leaving for the Vietnam war. My father did not give his blessings. Instead, my father told him to wait until he returned from the war and if we still felt the same for each other then he would give his blessings. Had I been engaged to him while he was gone, I would have waited faithfully for him. He was a God-fearing man with Jesus in his heart. But I did not wait. I pray he has forgiven me and that he went forward with a beautiful life. As for myself... my life's course was forever altered with the choices *I made* in my misdirected love and in my ignorance of God's Word.

I have no one to blame but myself. Without council in prayer, without seeking GOD's input, I floundered through life searching in vain for my one and only true soul mate! I am learning that I by myself can do nothing! I am nothing without GOD! His Word is opening my eyes that all things are possible to those that love Him and follow Him! All the glory belongs to GOD!

> **"*Jesus said, 'What is impossible with man is possible with GOD.'*" Luke 18:27** *(NIV)*

I now realize that believing I had enough love in each relationship to cover the both of us was also a self-righteous thought. More than that, it was a wrong thought. My love alone could not hold the broken unequally yoked relationships together. It takes three; it takes the love of Jesus in the middle to heal and restore. Only the love of Jesus can change hearts and save souls!

You may be asking yourself how I became unequally yoked in the first place? I'll tell you exactly how. I was lied to! I was deceived into believing that I was loved with the kind of devotional and unconditional love that I gave so easily and freely. I sought that kind of love from others with all my being. However, without the fruit of the Spirit of love one has nothing to give. Without the love of Jesus in one's hearts, how could one be faithful to me and how could one return my love? Unfortunately, I did not know of such things as the fruit of the Spirit either. And of course, without the fruit of love the truth in their heart always eventually became obvious.

There was one husband that would have been faithful, but my wounded soul could not "see" his heart. In my brokenness I let the enemy come between us and drive me away. I let him slip away from me for which I am truly sorry. I ask for his forgiveness too. He knows of whom I speak.

I believed I was supposed to obey my partner in life and be submissive to him, you know, to be dutiful and "ruled over." I was in bondage, chained by my perception of true love. With the love of Jesus in my heart, I had much love to give and give and give. Remember, the curses upon Eve were upon me. But as we have discussed, those curses have been broken. Jesus broke all curses when His tortured body hung upon the Cross. And as He bleed and died for us He freed us.

> *"You were bought at a price; do not become slaves of human beings." 1 Corinthians 7:23* (NIV)

I nearly lost my life looking for love that I already had. I did not know… I just did not know! I had been living on the milk of babes since childhood Sunday school!

> *"For everyone who partakes only of milk is unskilled in the word of righteousness, for he is a babe." Hebrews 5:13* (NKJV)

> *"But solid food belongs to those who are of full age, that is, those who by reason of use have their senses exercised to discern both good and evil." Hebrews 5:14* (NKJV)

God is gradually advancing me from the *milk* to the *solid food* of His Word. And Jesus is crushing all my wrong believing about the curses and lies that I have been living under in my state of ignorance. I pray my testimony may reach others with the message that it is not enough to be saved then coast through life carried in His arms as babies, content only with the milk of His Word. We must keep reading, studying and learning throughout our lifetime in order to learn of the mysteries of Jesus that are hidden in Scripture. That is the only way to achieve a personal one-on-one relationship with Jesus and arm ourselves against the murderous attempts and lies of Satan.

Spiritual blindness hindered my spiritual growth which led me to poor decisions allowing my free will to get me into distress. That truly is so very sad! But, as my research continues, I am growing. As I grow, Satan tries harder and harder to prevent publication of these books. I have had a multitude of problems with my electronic equipment, weird and bizarre issues. And then there are the multitude of distractions to take me away from writing. But Jesus has always come through. This book will indeed come to fruition by the grace of GOD Almighty for it was He that instructed me to write it. It is His book; therefore, He will get it completed and published. All the glory to GOD!

In the book of Job, Job expressed my own feelings when he repented after his eyes were opened to his self-righteous thinking that he knew the ways of GOD.

"I have heard of you by the hearing of the ear,
But now my eye sees You.
Therefore I abhor myself,
And repent in dust and ashes."
Job 42:5-6 (NKJV)

Thank you, Heavenly Father, for Jesus. Thank you, for the Sovereignty of Your Word, so full of knowledge and wisdom to guide me through the rest of my life.

Thank you, Jesus, for coming into my heart when I was just 3 ½ years of age. Thank you for Your love and for paying my sin debt! I pray for Your guidance daily that I may walk in your Holy presence.

Nanette Crapo 03/27/2019

"One thing I know, I was blind but now I see!"
<u>John 9:25</u> (NIV)

∘ ∘ ∘

"Of what value is an idol, since a man has carved it? Or an image that teaches lies? For he who makes it trusts in his own creation; he makes idols that cannot speak." "But the LORD is in His holy temple; let all the earth be silent before Him." <u>Habakkuk 3:18 & 20</u> (NIV)

∘ ∘ ∘

Chapter 4
Idolatry

∘ ∘ ∘

"Nevertheless I have this against you, that you have left your first Love." <u>Revelation 2:4</u> (NKJV)

No one prevented me from seeking GOD's Word on my own. I was just too busy impatiently trying to find my soul mate, pridefully "fixing" everything, foolishly stealing GOD's money, and ignorantly worshiping idols! It shames and pains me to expose all these horrific shortcomings and sins about myself, but it is what it is... my testimony. I fear many people, like myself, are also guilty of some if not all of these sins without knowing it. I pray if this is true that my testimony, however embarrassing and brutally honest it is, may open the eyes of others that they may see their own true selves.

The following explains how the devil utilized the curses upon Eve to redirect my love and desire from GOD to the men in my life. I take the blame for my unawareness thus I take the responsibility for the consequences as well. It is only by GOD's grace and mercy that my forty-year journey did not end my life at the hands of evil men. Men that knowingly or unknowingly follow a different master called Satan, *preying upon my loneliness as I searched for my souls mate. He knew I was lonely and used it as a weapon against me.*

"And the LORD God said, 'It is not good that man should be alone; I will make him a helper comparable to him." <u>Genesis 2:18</u> (NKJV)

The real enemy here is the devil. He can and will exploit our *fruit of the Spirit* and work them against us if we do not guard them. The *fruit of the Spirit* are gifts from GOD. (Galatians Chapter 5). God even says there are not any laws against such attributes. They are good *fruit* to have. They are the strengths of our character. We are to seek others with this *fruit of the Spirit* for they are of GOD. Had I known about the fruit of the Spirit I definitely would have recognized those that were of GOD and those that were not! Here is a list in case you are not familiar with them.

They are as follows:

- *love,*
- *peace,*
- *joy,*
- *gentleness,*
- *goodness,*
- *longsuffering (patience),*
- *faith,*
- *meekness, and*
- *temperance (self-control).*

Those I had chosen to give my love to had *no joy, no happiness, no patience, no meekness, no peace, no goodness, no self-control, and no love.* That can only mean one thing... they did not have *faith* in Jesus either! Whew, that is *all* of the *fruits* listed! No wonder those relationships were doomed before they ever started. No wonder GOD kept screaming at me "NO! Not that one either! Be patient! Wait for My choice for you!"

He was, you know. GOD was letting me see glimpses of their true character before the relationships got too far along, but I chose to ignore the warning bells. In fact, I not only ignored the warning signs, I was drawn further into the relationships because of the warning signs. Let me explain further... they had none of the fruit (fruit I was not aware of). I mistook their lack of joy and their sadness for loneliness. My compassionate heart was drawn to what I thought their need was... someone to love them. Someone like me with lots and lots of love to give and a strong desire to be needed and loved in return. LOL! I was duped... over and over again! Thus the ruts around my personal mountain of loneliness and despair!

My love was not what they needed. They needed the *fruit of the Spirit* which only comes when one believes and accepts Jesus into ones heart by faith. Then, and only then, does one receive such *fruit* through His Holy Spirit that dwells within us!

> *"Thus, by their fruit you will recognize them."*
> <u>Matthew 7:20</u> (NIV)

But, alas, I could not hear the warning bells through the noise of my own thoughts. I thought they needed me based upon what I wanted (to be needed), not what GOD was telling me. Definitely not the will of GOD for me, but my will which was based upon lies of the devil and curses of old.

Only Jesus can fill the emptiness in one's heart. It was unfortunate, but I have discovered that their emptiness is exactly what attracted me to them. I felt empathy because I too was so unhappy in my aloneness. I identified with the devastation of feeling unloved and unwanted and my heart went out to them. I only wanted to make them happy with my love so that they would love me in return. See how twisted that is? I was trying to be a bandage for someone that needed Jesus and all I had to offer was myself, a broken crutch. When they leaned on me we both fell.

Alas, I could not reach them because it just does not work that way. How does it work? I could not tell you the answer to that in January of 2019, but I can answer you now. We all need to draw near to Jesus Christ by seeking Him in the Word of GOD!

Each scripture that correlates to my life's journey, my testimony, is drawing me closer and closer to Jesus with clarity. I pray for everyone to experience this growth for themselves. It is truly an awesome and breathtaking journey; the ride of my life! Each day is a day of discovery of more of the mysteries between the pages, mysteries about Jesus Christ.

I cannot get enough. (I repeat certain things to stress a point in cash you, the reader, miss the point the first or second time like I have been known to do. It is not meant to insult anyone's intelligence.)

How embarrassing it is now to realize that I was subordinate to their rule over me. I was standing in their shadow, just breathing and keeping the thoughts in my head to myself for I knew my opinions did not matter to them. In addition to being seen and not being heard, I was sometimes feeling invisible. That is another thought the devil planted early on in my head, the thought of being invisible, of no importance. I was extremely shy and did not know what to say anyway. I blindly and willingly submitted myself to the domination of man rather than to the will of GOD!

The blind devotion I had for them was idol worship! Oh how far I had sunk into the devil's pit of deception in my ignorance! Instead of a capital "L" on my forehead for "Looser" I must have had a capitol "N" for "Needy". I was so starved for love and acceptance that I overlooked being unequally yoked, telling myself that I had enough love for both of us. I know... right? Talk about foolish self-righteousness; I did not even know how to love myself. All I knew for a certainty was that they loved themselves, and or money and material things more than they ever loved me or the women they left me for.

Remember, I do not speak of all my relationships. Regardless, those I do speak of... well, they all know of whom I speak. I will not name names or point fingers for none of it matters any more. And after all, I am as much (if not more) to blame as anyone for going against the will of GOD!

> *"Be not unequally yoked together with unbelievers: for what fellowship has Righteousness with unrighteousness: and what communion has light with darkness?" <u>2 Corinthians 6:14</u>* (KJV)

Without the light of Jesus one definitely walks in darkness. I have been told that there is nothing after death... just a black empty void of nothingness! Oh! How sad to know what they are headed for because they do not listen and do not believe in Jesus as the Son of GOD! I will continue to pray for their eternal souls. I pray that God remove the veil of disbelief from their eyes! Why would I do that? Because of the compassion and love from within the depth of the heart that GOD has blessed me with. Whatever they did to me is insignificant compared to the possibility of their souls suffering in hell for eternity! I do not and would not wish that eternal torment on anyone! But sometimes all one can do is pray.

In addition to all the above, I am learning that it is not up to me to "lead" or "save" the nonbeliever. I am to tell them of the plan of salvation, the gospel of Jesus Christ. How could I, a blind goose, lead anybody without the knowledge to do so?

> *"He also told them this parable: 'Can a blind man lead a blind man? Will they not both fall into a pit?"* **Luke 6:39** *(NIV)*

I was naive enough to think that everyone is capable of loving another person and all I had to do was try harder to win that love! However, love is a gift from GOD as one of the fruits of the Spirit and cannot be earned. A person will love you or not. A person will love Jesus or not. The choice is theirs to make, not mine. Like I said, it is not up to me to "save" or "lead" anyone to Christ. It is up to me to be a witness and plant seeds about the gospel of Jesus Christ and the rest is between them and Jesus. Sad as it is to say, I did not know how to do that either!

> *"How do you know, wife, whether you will save your husband? Or, how do you know, husband, whether you will save your wife?"* **1 Corinthians 7:16** (NIV)

After spending time in a psych ward for severe depression, anxiety, and an "imminent" nervous breakdown in the mid 80's, I became less and less able to "stay and fight" for a one-sided relationship. I do not condemn, nor do I condone marriage or divorce, for as you should realize by now I am still learning about what GOD has to say regarding both.

> *"And what agreement has the Temple of GOD with idols? for you are the Temple of the Living GOD; as GOD has said, I will dwell in them, and walk in them; and I will be their GOD, and they shall be My people."*
> <u>2 Corinthians 6:16</u> (KJV)

Following my self-will and being unequally yoked led me into the sin of idolatry again, and again! I was trying to please others by putting their needs and wants first in my life. I was giving them all my income (*GOD's money*) and all my love. You might say that I was trying to buy their love. Looking back I might say that as well, although I did not realize it at the time (spiritual blinders). I did everything willingly out of my desire to please and to be loved. The money did not mean anything to me without their love. True love is all I ever desired, but it eluded me time and again.

> *"...thou shalt love thy neighbor as thyself."*
> <u>Matthew 22:39</u> (KJV)

..."*thy neighbor as thyself*"; not with all your love and definitely not as GOD. Do not worship your spouse, your children, your money, your house, your car, or your anything! Make GOD first in your heart... always! Love and honor your spouse, do not place them equal to or above GOD! No matter how you look at *it* and no matter how you may try to justify *it*, *it* is what *it* is... ***idol worship!***

> *"Wherefore, my dearly beloved, flee from idolatry."*
> <u>1 Corinthians 10:14</u> (KJV)

Section 2

Surrendering "Old Man" Self

○ ○ ○

"that you put off, concerning your former conduct, the old man which grows corrupt according to the deceitful lusts, and be renewed in the spirit of your mind, and that you put on the new man which was created according to God, in true righteousness and holiness." Ephesians 4:22-24 (NKJV)

"Therefore, if anyone is in Christ, he is a new creation; old things have passed away; behold, all things have become new." 2 Corinthians 5:17 (NKJV)

❖ ❖ ❖

"Do not give dogs what is sacred; do not throw your pearls to pigs. If you do, they may trample them under their feet, and turn and tear you to pieces."
Matthew 7:6 (NIV)

❖ ❖ ❖

Chapter 1
Downward Spiral

○ ○ ○

I compare the previous forty years as being alone in a wilderness, circling a mountain. It was a mountain of dejection, rejection and suppression that I kept circling with each relationship. I could not climb it by myself though not for lack of trying. Instead, I was on a downward spiral into a dark pit of depression. Keep in mind this was before learning I could ask for help from GOD about anything and everything. This was during the time I thought that asking GOD for anything was selfish! And this was during the years of wandering in a fog of ignorance (a fog of my own doing), a fog that Jesus carried me through until He brought me back to the *ninety-nine*.

> *"If a man has a hundred sheep, and one of them goes astray, does he not leave the ninety-nine and go to the mountains to seek the one that is straying?"*
> <u>Matthew 18:12</u> (NKJV)

Each relationship made me strive to *not* repeat the same mistakes. Only one problem... I was still blind as to what those mistakes were. I assumed there was something wrong with me, and of course, there was. I just did not have a clue as to what that *something* was. I was still living without the wisdom of His Word, spending everything I had in an effort to buy love. So, what's the problem? It was not my money; it was and is GOD's money. GOD blessed me with the skills and the abilities to earn what money I had.

I really did not know anything about that at the time. I thought giving money at church was to help pay the church bills and since I did not belong to a church, I did not need to worry about it... right? Wrong! When I tithe the first 10%, He will bless the rest. If I do not tithe the first fruits, He does not bless the rest. It as simple as that! GOD does not curse it as in the Old Testament, but He does not bless it either. And if it is not blessed... well, it just seems to slip through my fingers. Seems there was never enough no matter how much I made. That is how I understand it to be. How He does it is beyond my comprehension, yet I believe. I now trust Him with the first fruits and my finances have truly been blessed.

Do not ask me how it works because GOD's ways are mysterious and beyond my scope of understanding. I can say that He has promised to open heaven and pour His blessings out upon us, (Malachi Chapter 3) and as I have already covered in Scripture, GOD cannot lie. I have *tested* Him on this as He has told me to do in His Word. (Malachi 3:10) Mysteriously, I always have more than enough... just saying. GOD is awesome!

> *"'Bring the whole tithe into the storehouse, that there may be food in my house. Test me in this,' says the LORD Almighty, 'and see if I will not throw open the floodgates of heaven and pour out so much blessing that you will not have room enough for it.'"* <u>Malachi 3:10</u> (NIV)

That being said, it now makes sense to me why my financial status was also in a downward spiral. I had only given tithes during the few years that I attended church. Instead, I spent all that I had on gifts for those I loved. I was trying to lift them up and make them happy with material things of this world. But, the more I bought, the more, bigger and better stuff they expected.

Work, eat, sleep, play in the garden and repeat the cycle. That was my life of solitude even in marriage. If they were happy I was happy, so deluded was I in my lonely misery. It was all about me trying to fix them with stuff while proving my love for them. How ridiculous it that? I am nothing. Only Jesus can fix them with His Love because Jesus is Love! Jesus is Agape!

My life was in a vicious cycle of distractions that lured me farther and farther away from my true heart's desire, Jesus Christ. I found myself trapped in the deceit and control of another again and again, relationship after relationship! And now I find out that I have been *robbing* GOD by not giving Him the first fruits of the money He allowed me to earn! All "my money" is not really my money at all. It all actually belongs to GOD!

> *"Will a mere mortal rob GOD? Yet you rob me. But you ask, 'How are we robbing you?' In tithes and offerings."* <u>Malachi 3:8</u> (NIV)

Eventually the gifts did not matter, and they became bored with me, I guess, as I was never really given a reason as to why they could not love me. Maybe they never really did? Anyway, I have been rejected for women much younger than myself more than once! That goes a long was in destroying one's self-confidence! However, I have since learned that GOD says *I am "fearfully and wonderfully made"*! I will keep repeating that verse, until it sinks into my heart so that I never forget it! You can do the same.

> *"I will praise Thee; for I am fearfully and wonderfully made; marvelous are Thy works; and that my soul knoweth right well."* <u>Psalm 139:14</u> (KJV)

Remember... GOD cannot lie, and He cannot take back His Word, His promises. Once spoken, His word will come to fruition. Just look in Genesis. GOD spoke the whole world and everything in it into existence. Besides, He has sworn it to us. It is written that GOD said:

> *"I have sworn by Myself; the Word has gone out of My mouth in righteousness, and shall not return, that unto me every knee shall bow, every tongue shall swear."* <u>Isaiah 45:23</u> (KJV)

How, you ask, has His Word gone out of His mouth? His spoken Word is written just as He spoke it. It was written by those that He anointed through His Holy Spirit.

> *"For the prophecy came not in old time by the will of man; but holy men of GOD spake as thy were moved by the Holy Ghost."* <u>2 Peter 1:21</u> (KJV)

GOD's Word is exactly as it says... His Word, His breathed Word, His actual breath. GOD still speaks to us through the Holy Spirit if we seek Him and listen. GOD is faithful in His Word, His Promise, as long as we remain faithful. Of that I can give my testimony as being a witness thereof in the writing of this book. It is not of myself that these thoughts came! They came as I searched, learned, and gained understanding about myself, my shortcomings, my sins through Holy Spirit that dwells within me! After all, I did ask Him, "Why" in prayer and the answers are still coming. I had no idea I had so many faults due to disobedience born out of ignorance!

It is very hard to explain to those who have not experienced it, but Holy Spirit is "guiding" me as I write. Only believers with a personal relationship with Jesus will understand how that is possible. But, believe me, it is the most awesome experience one can have! I am humbled by it all!

> *"All scripture is GOD-breathed and is useful for teaching; rebuking, correcting and training in righteousness,"* <u>2 Timothy 3:16</u> (NIV)

All the glory belongs to GOD! The Holy Spirit of Jesus lives within me. Yes, He "lives"! He is very much alive, and He speaks to my heart! It is up to me to listen!

I do not cry for lost finances. No, I am a cheerful giver, always have been. The problem has been that I have been an irresponsible giver. I did not even set aside anything for myself. The consequences of financial ruin descended upon me and escalated during my downward spiral until I was left destitute; not once, but twice over the past forty years. Twice I was left with all the bills and had no choice but to file bankruptcy. I sought financial advice from a credit counselling agency on both occasions. They laughed that I actually thought they could help me! Both times it was suggested to me that I file for bankruptcy. So, twice I had to go before a judge in humiliation feeling like the thief I was.

An important lesson I am now learning is how to become debt free by being more responsible with the money GOD has graced me with. To begin with I have to get out of debt by:

1: tithe 10%;
2: pay off all charge accounts, credit cards and loans;
3: stop charging stuff;
4. pay cash (0% interest!); and
5. save for the future.

On with the saga of the downward spiral! Repeating the same pattern around the same mountain eventually led me to violent men, not once but three times. The kind I had only seen on murder mystery shows. I lost absolutely everything each time except my life. Even so, I did not learn to stop being so trusting. That was and is very hard to do with a heart too soft and a will too strong. I am not complaining as I cannot imagine my heart being hard and without love. And for the record, I cannot complain about my self-will either, except to myself.

I do not understand those that lack compassion! GOD fearing, GOD loving men would never have even thought of doing such murderous and cowardly deeds to me or anyone else! I simply find it incomprehensible how a heart can only take and take and take some more, then discard without ever giving anything in return. The main thing, or the main lesson learned here was not to mistrust my heart, but instead, to *search* into their heart for the *fruit of the Spirit of love*.

> *"Everyone who loves has been born of God and knows God. Whoever does not love does not know God, because God is love."* <u>*1 John 4:8*</u> (NIV)

I had never heard of the *fruit of the Spirit* in Sunday school or Church! The depth of my ignorance was truly shameful! Three times I even gave my heart to men so full of dark hatred and evil intentions as to attempt to take my life, and once, the life of my eldest son and daughter-in-law!

> *"A righteous man cares for the needs of his animal, but the kindest acts of the wicked are cruel."* <u>*Proverbs 12:10*</u> (NIV)

The devil wants to *steal*, *kill*, and *destroy* one's life. Just be aware that he can and will use others to achieve that goals. But Jesus is for abundant life. All I can say is, "choose wisely".

> *"The thief does not come except to steal, and to kill, and to destroy, I have come that they may have life, and that they may have it more abundantly."* <u>*John 10:10*</u> (NKJV)

One of my disastrous relationships admitted, nonchalantly yet matter-of-factly, that he knew he had demons in him! You heard me right, though at the time I could not believe it either! GOD was there and He heard him too! *For it is written:*

> *"...even though no one is with us, remember that GOD is a witness between you and me." Genesis 31:50 (NIV)*

How was I so blind that I missed what is so obvious to me now? Oh, there were signs alright. Signs I would have recognized as such had I not had spiritual blinders on! God was definitely trying to warn me, to tell me to stay away from the *stranger*, but I could not hear Him as I did not yet know His voice. Plus, He warned me in Scripture:

> *"Lest thou give thine honour unto others, and thy years unto the cruel: Lest strangers be filled with thy wealth; and thy labours be in the house of a stranger." Proverb 5: 9-10 (KJV)*

That certainly describes my backsliding years! I literally gave my honor away (freely), wasted my years in the presence of *cruel* men, lost my wealth to *strangers* and labored in the house of *strangers*. Strangers is an appropriate analogy as their true identity was hidden from me until it was almost too late. But I do not look back with regret. I can move forward and use my mistakes to warn others. Hopefully, others will see themselves in my story and wake up before being totally devastated emotionally, financially and possibly even physically by *strangers*.

It still baffles me how anyone can reject the free gift of eternal life for the fun and games of the here and now! It appears that the gates of hell have been opened! Be on high alert and consider yourselves warned! Evil is ramped and we all need a Savior. Jesus is the Only Way to Father GOD and to life eternal.

> *"Jesus saith unto him, 'I am the way, the truth, and the life; no man cometh unto the Father, but by me." John 15:6 (KJV)*

There is only one Savior... Jesus! Seek Him for time is running out and the consequences of missing out on salvation is eternal death for one's soul. I will not sugar coat this for it is too important. Jesus *is* the only way to receive eternal life.

> *"But whoever fails to find Me harms himself; all who hate Me love death."* **Proverbs 8:36** (NIV)

There is spiritual evil in the supernatural warfare that surrounds us all. You can ask GOD to open your spiritual eyes to let you see into the supernatural world around you; but I do not advise that you ask. GOD has called me to give my testimony as a witness into the dark realm of the supernatural, so you do not have to see the horrific sights that were revealed to me. I pray you open our spiritual ears and hear what GOD would have me tell you through this book.

Have I mentioned that the *gifts of the Spirit* (1 *Corinthians 12: 8-10*) differ from the *fruit of the Spirit*? They are discussed at length in my first book. Discerning spirits is one of those gifts. Thankfully, it is not a constant gift. I cannot image seeing the things I have seen on a constant daily basis! Instead it is given whenever GOD deems it is necessary, for whatever reason. Only He knows His reasons, but I venture to say that it is for our protection, to get our attention. Believe me when I tell you that He had my full undivided attention as he let me know that it was time for me to leave. I had been wavering about leaving a volatile relationship in spite of all the near accidents that could have ended my life. I still believed that there is good in us all. I know, I know, I was a hopeless, helpless, clueless (but needy) fool. I was beyond being an ignorant fool. I was just plain stupid now, and still blind! The cemetery if full of such as that!

So be careful what you ask GOD for! He allowed me to witness blue eyes turn solid black for about 5 seconds! Believe me, that is not what I thought I was asking for, but it got the job done! And once I saw the tongue of the serpent... terror of terrors! No, I was not drinking nor was I dreaming! I saw both just as clearly as I once saw dark fog-like entities swirling just below ceiling level over a patient that had just expired (passed away). I had never witnessed any of these things before and I pray to never witness them again!

In my first book ANGELS SPIRITS AND A 9MM SCREW: Legacy Of Faith And Love Through Five Generations, I have discussed them as *"shadow people"*. For the record, I believe they are evil entities, demons, minions of the devil, and that they never were "people". I mention them again now as dark fog-like entities in case you are not familiar with the sister book to this one.

Each sight, each manifestation, was more frightening than any horror movie I have ever seen. Somehow that patient knew at the moment of death that the darkness had come for them. And somehow they knew there was no escape! Will that be your fate? It does not have to be so! Jesus is waiting for you with His loving arms open wide! Run into His arms and receive salvation.

> *"If you declare with your mouth, Jesus is LORD, and believe in your heart that GOD raised Him from the dead, you will be saved."* Romans 10:9 (NIV)

GOD's legions of angels are in a constant supernatural battle with the devil and his demons in the spiritual realm that I mentioned! Although I have seen the dark entities and cannot unsee them, I no longer fear the things that go "bump" in the night, because God is for me.

> *"What shall we then say to these things? If GOD be for us, who can be against us?"* Romans 8:31 (KJV)

I do not hate those that sought to destroy me. I very much have compassion for their lost souls. I have seen what is waiting to escort nonbelievers to their final eternal destination. I pray it is not too late for them to choose Jesus and that GOD have mercy upon them. At this point, that is all I can do for them from afar... pray.

The beginning of the end of the downward spiral was when I cried out to Jesus for help! It is by His grace that I am alive to give you my testimony even though Satan sought to pluck me from the hand of my Savior, Jesus Christ.

> *"And I give unto them eternal life; and they shall never perish, neither shall any man pluck them out of My hand." John 10:28* (KJV)

Yet, I am still here to praise Him and give Him all the glory for all the miracles and blessing He has showered my life with. I give thanks to Jesus daily for my salvation, for His protection and for His love. I give thanks to Father GOD for His love and for His mercies upon me which are made new daily. Without His grace and mercy upon me I would be condemned into eternal darkness. I would have succumbed to the darkness of depression a long, long time ago.

> *"It is of the LORD's mercies that we are not consumed, because His compassions fail not. They are made new every morning: Great is thy faithfulness." Lamentation 3:22-23* (KJV)

◦ ◦ ◦

"...I sinned, and perverted what was right, but I did not get what I deserved. He redeemed my soul from going down to the pit, and I will live to enjoy the light.'"
<u>*Job 33:27-28*</u> (NIV)

◦ ◦ ◦

CHAPTER 2

End Of Self

○ ○ ○

"Too long have I lived among those who hate peace. I am for peace; but when they speak, they are for war." **Psalm 121:6-7** (NIV)

The downward spiral continued until the inevitable happened. The emotional onslaught became physical, but, of course, it was an accident. My neck was jerked so violently that it sent me to the emergency room with what is called a "stinger" by football players. My nerves and muscles were overstretched leaving me with numbness of my right arm for days, and pain in the right side of my head for nearly three years! That should tell you how violently my head was jerked, "accidently" of course, but violently enough that it could have broken my neck! But for the grace of GOD's protection I survived with just a "stinger". Thank You Jesus for saving my life and protecting me from the paralysis of a broken neck or worse, death, at the hands of *"the violent man"*!

"Keep me O LORD, from the hands of the wicked; preserve me from the violent man; who have purposed to overthrow my goings." **Psalm 140:4** (KJV)

I could not file a police report even though I was afraid for my life! For one thing, I had no proof and no earthly witnesses. It would have been his word against mine. Secondly, and more importantly, there was much more than a "stinger" involved here. I can only divulge that the danger to my life was a real threat from unsavory "acquaintances" of the man that was in my life at the time; and none were children of GOD...

"For we wrestle not against flesh and blood, but against principalities, against powers, against the rulers of the darkness of this world, against spiritual wickedness in high places." Ephesians 6:12 (KJV)

They were mere puppets, lurking about, controlled by the evil puppet master. They were seeking to cause me harm with pure evil intentions. By staying in such a volatile situation, I was endangering myself by association.

"Whoso is partner with a thief hateth his own soul: ..." Proverbs 29:24 (KJV)

I have been deceived and betrayed over and over again because I am too hard-headed and too soft-hearted. My heart kept forgiving because I see the good in people. It was the evil staring me in the face that I refused to accept in my heart as reality. I made excuse after excuse for those I loved. That made me an enabler which actually encouraged their behavior. It not only encouraged their behavior, it made them push the envelope of my loving, giving nature. I truly believe that Satan was trying to break me through them. But GOD had other plans for me!

Those that walked in darkness were not the real enemy. They were but pawns and are to be pitied. Satan was the enemy. Satan was trying to chip away at the heart GOD gave me, the heart that man discarded and shattered. It nearly ended my life with an attempted suicide. Emotional pain manifested into physical pain and had been crushing my soul for forty years. The cause of my wounds remained as a scar upon my very soul. Jesus knows all about scars! My eternal soul rests in His nail-scared hands!

Well, obviously my attempt at suicide failed, (praise GOD) and my life did not end that day... but it did stop. I became stuck in limbo, unable to move forward for forty years. Lost in the foggy darkness of the depression of the past which was preventing me from seeing the hope of the future.

Though I did not realize it back then, Jesus was in that fog with me. He brought me back from that dark place with the light of His Love. He is carrying me now as He carried my cross at Calvary.

Jesus never left me. He has been with me every second, every step of those forty years of disobedience, and He is with me now! He will remain with me long after this book is finished. He will be with me throughout infinity. My journey with Jesus shall never end! Amen! I find the scope of His protection to be awesome! Believe me, GOD hears your sobs, your cries of despair when you have no words to describe the depth of your sorrow!

> *"In the same way the Spirit helps us in our weakness. We do not know what we ought to pray for, but the Spirit himself intercedes for us through wordless groans"* <u>Romans 8:26</u> (NIV)

I was unknowingly asking for help with my tears. GOD catches our tears and puts them in His bottle. He does not miss a single drop... awesome!

> *"You numbered my wanderings;*
> *Put my tears into Your bottle;*
> *Are they not in Your book?*
> *When I cry out to You,*
> *Then my enemies will turn back;*
> *This I know, because GOD is for me."*
> <u>Psalm 56:8-9</u> (NKJV)

That is a beautiful image to have in my mind. GOD sees my misery and catches my tears in a bottle because He cares, He loves me. Jesus loves me too. He really loves me, and He has never left me! I had not turned to Him because I did not know I could. I though it was selfishness to pray for onself. And I did not turn to anyone else because I was isolated and alone and did not think anyone cared enough to help me. The self-pity had definitely set in. Besides, I was used to fixing things myself and I was too embarrassed to show weakness. I am learning that is a form of pride!

Only readers that have suffered emotionally and psychologically, for whatever reason or cause, (that qualifies pretty much everyone) can understand the heaviness of profound depression that weighs down one's soul. Once the suffering is compounded over time, one is hindered from being able to just let go, and prevented from being able to move on.

The heaviness of intense hopeless depression, wondering if the pain will ever go away and wondering if one will be able to hang on for one more day, can destroy the joy in one's soul. I carried that pain for forty years and everything I did in an attempt to fix it only made matters worse and worse and worse... and even worse than that! I know that you know what I mean!

Even though I forgave those that betrayed me, the rejection of those betrayals had deepened my feelings of worthlessness and loneliness. That is what ravished my heart and gnawed at my soul, sucking the light out of my spirit. You would think that I would just accept it as my lot in life as it is all I can remember; being alone in the natural even though I knew Jesus was with me in the supernatural. But I needed someone to hold me and comfort me. I did not realize Jesus can do that too if I would just let him!

So here I was, completely broken from a lifetime of chasing after the desires of my heart (*a soul mate*) and letting nonbelievers dominate and rule over me (*curses of Eve*). Here I was, once again thrown away and forgotten like a shattered piece of pottery.

> *"I am forgotten as a dead man out of mind: I am like a broken vessel."* <u>**Psalm 31:12**</u> (KJV)

God has been working on me to put the past in the past because I have been stuck there for far too long! The forty-year burden of a broken heart and shattered soul had brought me to a state of complete broken helplessness. This "state" allowed me to knowingly and willingly cry out for help for the first time in my life. The cry that Jesus had been patiently waiting to hear from me for over forty years. A cry admitting that I was at the *end of self*.

> *"My son, do not despise the LORD's discipline and do not resent His rebuke, because the LORD disciplines those He loves, as a father the son he delights in."* **Proverbs 3:11-12** *(NIV)*

The sooner we wake up, take responsibility for our poor choices of disobedience, repent, and give everything over to GOD... the better. I pray my testimony may save others from such a lengthy period of suffering the consequences of self-destructive disobedience.

I truly believe this book has the anointing of Heavenly Father to give me healing through understanding of the knowledge of His wisdom. I also truly believe and pray that others can learn from these Scriptures, can apply them to their own lives, and can receive their own healing as we journey together.

> *"Do not be wise in your own eyes; fear the LORD and shun evil."* **Proverbs 3:7** (NIV)

My expectations then, as now, is that Jesus is listening and always will be. Of my three best friends in this life thus far, Jesus is my closest. **Janet Chalk Payton Sanders**, my best friend since 5th grade, moved far away. My sister and best friend, **Sharon Crapo Chrysafis**, moved even farther away... all the way to Greece! Only Jesus remains with me 24/7. I knew that I could talk to Him anywhere and anytime, about anything and everything. I knew He could hear me and that He loved me. That always gave me a certain amount of comfort.

However, I never expected an answer, so I was not listening for one! I talked *to* Him but not *with* Him. There is a vast world of difference as I have learned. But, at the time, I did not know how to ask for help from anyone, especially from GOD. I just did not know... almost famous last words! Praise GOD for His patience, mercy and grace!

If you are a believer in GOD's plan of salvation and you have accepted Jesus Christ as your Savior, but you are now a backslider for whatever reason, you are still covered by GOD's grace and mercy and cannot lose your salvation. However, that does not mean He will not keep you from suffering the consequences of your bad decisions. Ask me, I know first-hand. I was to blame for all I went through, and I know it could have been far worse had Jesus not been there with me fighting my battles! On the other hand, it could have been far better had I been living in His Word.

GOD knows our hearts. He protected me from death at the hands of evil. He thwarted every move against me for He knew even before they did what they were up to. I tried to tell them that, but they did not believe. I remember saying defiantly, "*I am a child of GOD and when you mess with me you are messing with GOD and GOD always wins!*"

That was so prophetic though I did not realize it at the time. Prophetic because it was, is, and always will be so true! I had said it just hours before crouching in fear for my very life. Even though I said the words, I had quickly forgotten them in my confusion and fear while trying to figure out what to do to get myself out of the danger I found myself in!

> *"For a man's ways are in full view of the LORD, and He examines all his paths." Proverbs 5:21* (NIV)

The supernatural war between good and evil surrounded me in the spiritual realm. No way one can fight that spiritual war without Jesus! I thank GOD that He was fighting all my spiritual battles even while my head was hidden in the sand. Without the Word of GOD as my armor I was just not prepared to survive on my own efforts. I was as helpless as a newborn! I had been living in a self-created bubble of self-reliance just to be brought to my knees in utter defeat! There I was, a completely broken vessel on my knees, in the floor, in the dark, in the middle of the night, in complete terror. That is when I had my *awakening,* my "*Damascus moment*" with Jesus!

He was right there in a flash! He had been waiting for me to give up being independent and becoming dependent upon Him and trusting in Him with the innocent trusting faith that I had as a child. Instead of continuing with my pity parties and crying "*Why?*", "*What did I do wrong?*", "*All I did was love him!*", "*Why can't anyone return my love?*"; I finally turned my focus to Jesus. My mother's battle cry filled the room as I surrendered my *old man self...* **"JESUS! Please help me!"**

> *"'Because he loves me,' says the LORD, 'I will rescue him; I will protect him, for he acknowledges my name.'"*
> **Psalm 91:14** (NIV)

◦ ◦ ◦

"Cast your cares on the LORD and He will sustain you; He will never let the righteous fall." Psalm 55:22 (NIV)

◦ ◦ ◦

CHAPTER 3
Damascus Moment With Jesus

○ ○ ○

> *"Do not remember the sins of my youth and my rebellious ways; according to your love remember me, for you, LORD are good.* <u>Psalm 25:7</u> (NIV)

I thought if I loved someone that they would love me in return! What kind of thinking it that? I'll tell you... it's foolish thinking, wrong thinking, and dangerous thinking! After all that had happened throughout my life, I had thought that the kind of danger I suddenly found myself in only happened in the movies or to other people by other people... didn't it? All I now knew was that it was time to wake up to the reality of the evil surrounding me or perish! It was time to cry out for help or die!

"I am now so frightened and so threatened by pure evil that it is taking every fiber of my waning courage to sit and wait all alone in the darkness for that evil to break down the door and surge in on me. I have no plan, no help and no hope. I am not depressed, not this time; at least not yet. I am too afraid for that emotion. Fear consumes me. I changed the locks out on the front and the back doors with shaking hands lest I not get them installed in time. I made sure the windows were locked! I hung sheets and towels over all the windows!

I spent the rest of the day trying to figure out a plan. Everything I think of has a negative spin on it; making me think it will not work out. There is no one I can call as I have been alienated from my family and the few friends I used to have, except the one in Tennessee; but that is too far away, and I have no vehicle of my own. More ways that he is controlling me. I am a prisoner, without hope for escape. I cannot call the local authorities as I have no witnesses for my defense, no evidence against them to prove how they have sought to end my life. I cried out, "JESUS! Please help me! I don't know what to do! I can't fix this!"

(Taken from the journals of Nanette Crapo)

"JESUS! Please help me!" That was my mother's battle cry. On this particular day, it became mine! I was crouched in fear for my life with a gun in one hand for protection. The gun truly was useless against the darkness that was seeking to extinguish my light. I was at the point of not being able to bear anymore, completely broken and shattered. I, I, I... I am nothing of myself! I finally realized how helpless I truly was as I ended one season of my life and entered another. This season with Jesus was definitely a significant turning point. I have had four major encounters with Jesus since my birth. I will list them in chronological order:

- The first was finding faith in Jesus at age 3 and ½.
- The second was accepting Jesus as my LORD and Savior and being baptized at age 15.
- The third was baptism in the Holy Spirit at age 45.
- The fourth was totally surrendering to Jesus at age 65.
  - My Damascus moment...

Jesus has been trying to talk to me through His Holy Spirit that dwells within me. Oh, how much time I have lost in my deafness of disobedience! Finally, I not only heard Him, I heard Him with clarity and understanding when He simply said, *"Read Psalms".* It was the beginning of the end of my heartache and loneliness.

> *"Thy hands have made me and fashioned me; give me understanding, that I may learn they commandments."*
> **Psalm 119:73** (KJV)

It is sad that my physical life had to be jeopardized before I woke up and came to the end of me, myself and I. I felt totally alone and hopeless in my terrified situation with evil prowling outside in the darkness. After about an hour of crying in abject terror, in a puddle of tears, in the middle of the night, in the middle of the floor with a gun in one hand (for my protection)... I heard my mother's plea come from deep within my soul. I looked toward heaven and cried out loud, *"JESUS! Please help me! I don't know what to do! I can't fix this!"*

I did not realize it until later, but that was the moment of my total surrender to Jesus; like Saul (Paul) on the road to Damascus! (Acts 9: 3-7, which is coming up shortly.) I have not looked back. My faith and my total trust in Jesus is that He will meet all my needs, large and small! I have submerged myself in His Word thus beginning my journey! It began the moment I cried out to the name above all names... "JESUS"!

> *"Therefore GOD also has highly exalted Him and given Him the name which is above every name,"*
> *Philippians 2:9* (NKJV)

Whose name are you going to call when you have been brought to the end of self and find yourself on your knees in the middle of the road to Damascus? Sooner or later, everyone meets Jesus there. Why wait until then? Why go through the struggles of life on your own efforts, suffering the consequences of disobedience to GOD's will for you? Why not heed my testimony instead and save yourself much wasted time and misery?

Jesus' invitation is available to all; no if's, and's or but's. All you have to do is believe He is the Son of GOD, that He gave His life to cleanse you of your sins, confess your sins, and accept Him as your LORD and Savior. To accept Him is eternal life, but to reject Him is eternal torment in hell. Why wait and miss out on all the blessings He has for you?

You can call upon Jesus right now! You can invite Him into your heart and experience first-hand for yourself how truly beyond words His love for you really is! He is already closer than you realize. He can hear your heartbeat. He can hear your silent cries of anguish from deep within your soul, the cries no one else can hear. He is there with you now, in the dark loneliness of the night. His arms are open wide to hold you, to protect you and to love you. Jesus is waiting for you to come into His loving arms with the trusting faith and love of an innocent child. His blood will cleanse you, no matter what your story is. His love will make you cry tears of joy and you will never want to let Him go! And then you will wonder... "Why did I wait so long?"

For those of you who do not know the story of the Apostle Paul's (Saul's) personal encounter with Jesus on the road to *Damascus*, I will briefly tell you. Saul was a Jew with much authority. He was persecuting Christians because he did not believe Jesus was the promised Messiah, Christ. So one day on his way to Damascus to obtain permits to round up and persecute Christians... *he met Jesus... personally*!

> *"As he journeyed he came near Damascus, and suddenly a light shone around him from heaven. Then he fell to the ground, and heard a voice saying to him, 'Saul, Saul, why are you persecuting me?' And he said, 'Who are You, Lord?' Then the Lord said, "I am Jesus, whom you are persecuting."'* <u>Acts 9:3-5</u> (NKJV)

Saul became one of the greatest apostles and preached to both Jews and gentiles (non-Jews). Awesome encounter and worth reading. The Bible is full of awesome stories worth reading. I am sure you will find yourself in some of them.

Now that is what you call a one-on-one personal encounter with Jesus! It was at such a time that I surrendered my will to Him! He immediately answered me, within the twinkling of an eye! To my shocked surprise, I heard Him! Not out loud but in my thoughts. He simply said, *"Read Psalms"*. I knew it was Jesus because He was calm and because I was not! And in my panicked state of mind the furthermost thing on my mind was reading. I thought the Bible was just a book about yesteryear... thousands of yesteryears! GOD was about to introduce me to His

Living Word, Jesus Christ, as I had never seen Him before, through the pages of The Holy Bible!

"In my distress I cried unto the LORD, and He heard me." Psalm 120:1 (KJV)

There was no urgency in Him. It did not surprise me that He was calm. He took charge, after all He Is GOD. However, there sure was urgency within me! I jumped up as if struck with lightening! Funny that thought came to me, as I can imagine that Saul may have thought he had been struck with lightening when he saw the *"light from Heaven"*.

Anyway, I literally ran to my bedside table, grabbed my dusty 50-year-old Bible and ran back to the safety of my post. My post was situated to where I could see the front and the back door, on guard for intruders, lest they sneak up on me if I dozed off. I was huddled in the floor, sandwiched in between the huge ottoman and the sofa. This served as my fortress in case of a spray of bullets or something. I was indeed terrified, and my imagination was not helping matters. My imagination was well founded though, based on who and what may be lurking outside! The devil was compounding my anxiety with fear by the moment! It took a few minutes to find the book of Psalms. I had to look at the table of contents! This I confess, to my ignorance and shame!

The next three days and nights were spent huddled in the floor with my gun (for protection), and my dusty bible. Looking back I can clearly see that all I really needed for protection was my bible. It was a gift from Church when I was baptized at age fifteen (15). It was in pristine condition for lack of use. I was thumbing through it now, looking for the book of Psalms. I can just imagine GOD slowly shaking His head at me for thinking I still needed that gun when He was now in charge.

I could almost recite to you Psalms, the 23rd chapter, from my memories as a child in vacation bible school; however, to my shame I did not know the number of the chapter (23). So, I started flipping through the whole book of Psalms frantically searching for it. After doing that for about five minutes GOD spoke again, not out loud, but deep within me. He calmly reminded me He did not specify Psalms 23 and was now telling me to start at the beginning and "read Psalms". I remember thinking to myself, *"that's a good idea, why didn't I think of that?"*

GOD was now speaking to me through the same Holy Spirit that has been with me all those years, guiding and warning me with that sixth sense thing. But, I could not hear Him as I now can because my ears were plugged in my state of disobedience. So... this time I heard Him and started reading at Psalm 1:1. In other words, I obeyed GOD. And once again I can just imagine GOD slowly shaking His head at my continued panicked and confused state of mind because He had already set His plan in motion! In fact, I am learning that His plan was set into motion long before I was even born, and He already knows the outcome. Awesome!!! And GOD knew how much I could bear so as soon as I ask, He showed me the way to escape!

> *"No temptation has seized you except what is common to man. And God is faithful; He will not let you be tempted beyond what you can bear. But when you are tempted, He will also provide a way out so that you can stand up under it."* <u>*1 Corinthians 10:13*</u> (NIV)

Over the course of those three days and nights I was on a forced fasting while reading, dozing off for a few minutes at a time from sheer exhaustion, and reading some more. There was nothing in the house to drink except water. There was no bread, only food that required cooking, which I was not about to do. Nor was I about to turn on any lights! Did I mention that I was reading at night by flashlight? I gave thanks to Father GOD at the time that there were several at my disposal. So, I drank water and read Psalms, and read Psalms, and read some more Psalms. Psalms is the only book in <u>The Holy Bible</u> that I read during those three days, over and over again as per His instructions.

This was my first intentional act of obedience to Father GOD, now that I knew what He wanted me to do.

I was trusting Him totally and depending upon Him totally. Comfort and peace descended upon me as God's word entered into my mind then into my heart, giving me understanding that I sorely lacked. Jesus really was speaking directly to me through Scripture.

Looking back in my mind I can envision Jesus there with me as I sat huddled in fear. I began to feel like a child sitting in the lap of Jesus with His loving arms around me, holding the book in front of me and reading to me. Of course, I realize now that was exactly what He was doing! Don't ask me how I know... I just know. It was another wonderous miracle! Jesus was right there with me as I have always known He was.

> *"... for HE hath said, I will never leave thee, nor forsake thee." Hebrews 13:5* (KJV)

My GOD is an Awesome GOD for sure. His Word gave me hope, peace and strength, just as He promised it would. Praise GOD! I do give all the glory to Heavenly Father. I knew I needed to leave long before it got to the point that it had gotten to. However, I was immobilized by insecurities and fears. The devil had me convinced that there was no way out, no vehicle, no money, nowhere to go, no one that cared; therefore, I might as well stay where I was... trapped in his pit of lies!

Just as I mentioned, GOD had a plan. He guided me every step of the way to safety revealing a little of the plan at a time, lest I become nervous and give myself away. GOD's plans were perfectly orchestrated and totally awesome! I was completely trusting Him and completely depending upon Him to get me out of the life-threatening danger that I had managed to get myself in with my own efforts! I had an immediate sense of relief to be giving my messed up life over to Jesus! Although I was still petrified, a sense of calm had already been activated in my soul!

> **"Our help is in the name of the LORD, who made heaven and earth."** Psalm 124:8 (KJV)

I gave my heart to Jesus at a very early age. I finally understood that there is so much more to Jesus. In order to have a personal relationship with Him, I needed to give all of me. Understanding of that knowledge, found in His Word, has allowed me to surrender my will to Him. Full surrender with full dependence upon Jesus is the Damascus moment that I have heard so much about but did not understand until it happened to me.

One has not fully surrendered if one is running amuck trying to fix and control everything in life, like me. It does not matter whether of good intentions or not, nor whether out of ignorance or not. Jesus is the only answer to anything and everything. And of course, He is the only way to Father GOD! Some lessons are hard learned… this one took me forty years! But, GOD has told me it is time to move on. Each day, each verse I read, is adding to the healing process since this journey with Jesus began. It has been several years, but I continue to seek His Word and draw ever closer each day. My quest for more knowledge of His Word will never end.

Jesus surrounds me with His unconditional love. I have prayed to Holy Spirit to align my will with the will of Father GOD so that I know what His will for me is. It is only when I know His will for me that I can be obedient and that is my desire. No longer do I presume to be self-righteous, for I will always fall short. Even though I know I fall far short of being able to walk as Jesus did, I will walk with Him until I see Him face to face. The good news is that Jesus covers my sins with His blood, and I do not wish to knowingly disappoint Him. So, I do not look at it like, *"I am forgiven so I can do whatever I want to do"*. It does not work like that.

My salvation is not a free ticket to continue to blatantly sin, even though Jesus loves me in spite of my sinful self. Holy Spirit lets me know when something I have said or done is wrong and that in turn makes me ask for forgiveness and want to be a better person. You know… putting away my old man self as my new self is transformed daily through Holy Spirit.

> "Guide me in your truth and teach me, for you are GOD my Savior, and my hope is in you all day long."
> **Psalm 25:5** (NIV)

Ignorance in the promises of GOD will put you at the mercy of the devil and he (the devil) will have you in the pit of self-pity and depression in a heartbeat.

Thought for today:

Satan will continue to attack with one goal in mind... to destroy one's soul! I personally believe that his #1 weapon of choice is depression through loss and loneliness which may ultimately lead one to suicide. The truth about Jesus and how much He loves us, found in the Word of GOD, is our only true defense against such attacks of dark, negative evil! The devil spares no one! We all need a Deliverer and a Protector! No other name has the Majestic power to make the enemy flee; no one but Jesus, Yeshua, Our Messiah!

From the journal of Nanette Crapo 03/21/2019

> *"Then the seventy returned with joy, saying, 'LORD, even the demons are subject to us in Your name.'"*
> **Luke 10:17** (NKJV)

Have you had a Damascus moment with Jesus? It is the moment when one realizes one is but an insignificant speck of dust blowing in a hurricane and helpless without Him. It is the moment that one realizes that Jesus is very much alive and that His Holy Spirit dwells within believers. It is the moment of one's total surrender to His Sovereign powers! It is only then that one can find peace and comfort in His protective arms and in His unending love. Don't be afraid of having your Damascus moment! It will change your life forever and totally blow your mind!

Nanette Crapo, April 5, 2019

*"When my soul fainted within me,
I remembered the LORD;
And my prayer went up to You,
Into Your holy temple."*
Jonah 2:7 (NKJV)

Section 3
Ask Seek Believe Find Trust

❖ ❖ ❖

"Ask, and it shall be given you; seek and ye shall find; knock and it shall be opened unto you." Mathew 7:7 (KJV)

"But the scripture hath concluded all under sin, that the promise by faith of Jesus Christ might be given to them that believe." Galatians 3:22 (KJV)

"Who walks in darkness and has no light? Let him trust in the name of the Lord and rely upon his God" Isaiah 50:10 (NKJV)

◦ ◦ ◦

"Have no fear of sudden disaster or of the ruin that overtakes the wicked, for the LORD will be at your side and will keep your foot from being snared."
Proverbs 3:25-26 (NIV)

◦ ◦ ◦

Chapter 1

Ask The Lion Of Juda

° ° °

> *"I wept and wept because no one was found who was worthy to open the scroll or look inside. Then one of the elders said to me, 'Do not weep! See, the Lion of the tribe of Judah, the Root of David, has triumphed. He is able to open the scroll and its seven seals.'"*
> <u>Revelation 5:4-5</u> (NIV)

"J*ESUS! Please help me!"* GOD did that! He pulled those words from the cobwebs of my memory because I was being overpowered by the evil accomplices of the devil that were outside *roaring like lions*.

> *"Be sober, be vigilant; because your adversary the devil, as a roaring lion, walketh about, seeking whom he may devour..."* <u>1 Peter 5:8</u> (KJV)

I had fallen to the floor with total surrender to Jesus in my Damascus moment. This chapter describes in detail the three days that were spent with the Lion of the tribe of Juda. I was literally face to face with Jesus though I could not see Him. It was the most intense, the most cherished and the most mind-blowing experience I had ever had to date. Hard to explain... surreal, but I wanted it to last forever! It was the beginning of the end of my downward spiral as Jesus took me out of the well-worn ruts around my self-made mountain of desolation, desperation and isolation.

"Nevertheless He saved them for His name's sake, That He might make His mighty power known." **Psalm 106:8** (NKJV)

Jesus is real, He is alive, and He is with me. Jesus hears everything I say, and He sees everything I do. It was true when I was 3 ½ years old, it is true now, and it will always be true.

"Jesus Christ is the same yesterday, today, and forever. Do not be carried about with various and strange doctrines. " **Hebrews 13:8-9** (NKJV)

I never doubted what my Grandpa Crapo told me, that Jesus Christ is always wherever I am... always. One of my most cherished moments in life is when there was a shift in the paradigm and I literally felt the arms of Jesus enveloping me.

All of a sudden, Jesus is moving down from ceiling level where He has been since my childhood, to floor level with me! He is suddenly here beside me, behind me and in front of me. He is totally surrounding me, and He is within me! I can physically feel His supernatural energy permeating the atmosphere in the instant it has taken me to cry out, "Jesus! Please help me! I don't know what to do! I can't fix this"! Things have changed from "sensing" He is here listening and watching over me to "feeling" His protective arms around me, and to "hearing" Him reading along with me! His powerful presence is filling the room, dissolving my fears, wiping away my tears, and defeating my enemies that are lurking outside in the dark!

(Taken from the journals of Nanette Crapo)

*"It shall come to pass
That before they call I will answer;
And while they are still speaking,
I will hear."*
<u>Isaiah 65:24</u> (NKJV)

You may be asking yourself, *"Why was Jesus up at the ceiling?"* Perhaps it was because my grandparents always looked up when talking about *"Baby Jesus"* so in my mind's eye I visualized Him "up there"? Or perhaps it was because I visualized Him in heaven instead of here with me? I really do not know, but of course, He wasn't *"up there"* at all! He was and is within me and will forever remain so. That was just my perception born out of my ignorance of not knowing about His Holy Spirit. Nothing, and I repeat, ***nothing can be compared to my personal encounter with Jesus, my Damascus moment***! He remains within me and Praise GOD, He did not go back up to the ceiling!

In the story "The Night the Holy Spirit Screamed" (in my first book) I have testified how the Holy Spirit of Jesus saved my life when I was eighteen years old by screaming for me. The scream came from deep within me when I was too traumatized to move or speak on my own. Even though my throat had closed from sheer terror, He used His breath in my lungs and made a sound I cannot duplicate, for I have tried.

It was a very loud, very deep throaty cry on my behalf from GOD's Holy Spirit within me. (Taken from: **ANGELS SPIRITS AND A 9 MM SCREW, Legacy of Love and Faith Through Five Generation** by Nanette Crapo.)

That is a night that I shall never forget! I look back upon it now with such awe because I did not realize at the time that the *Lion of Juda* was defending me from the intruder in the darkness of the night. I appreciate how awesome and supernatural the experience I had at age 18 really was when His loud terrifying cry shattered the silence in the darkness. The depth and the volume of His voice jolted me into action as I moved away from the intruder in the same instant that the intruder fled for his life!

> *"The wicked flee when no man pursueth; but the righteous are bold as a lion."* <u>Proverbs 28:1</u> *(KJV)*

That is the supernatural power of the *Lion of the tribe of Juda, Jesus.* (Revelation 5:5) He also watches over us as the good shepherd watches over his sheep.

> *"I am the good shepherd. The good shepherd gives His life for the sheep."* **John 10:11** (NKJV)

It is necessary that I include loads and loads of verses in this chapter because they changed my emotional state from one of abject terror to one of courageous indignation. I read them now with joy in my heart in remembrance of what Jesus saved me from. However, I do not rejoice over the downfall of my enemies. My heart grieves for them. They are but empty vessels without joy, without love, without hope and without Jesus. I cannot rejoice over that! The joy in my heart is because I am safe, and I have been freed from the bondage of abuse and fear through the precious Blood of Jesus Christ!

> *"For You have delivered me from death and my feet from stumbling, that I may walk before God in the light of life."* <u>Psalm 56:13</u> (NIV)

The roaring lions (my enemies) were outside seeking to destroy me. (1 Peter 5:8). But Jesus, the *Lion of Juda*, is greater than any ole' evil shriveled up toothless lion that lurks outside in the darkness of the night. Besides, I have heard somewhere that Jesus has him chained up and he cannot harm me as long as I stay in the shadow of my Protector.

O.K., grab yourself some sweet tea (add sugar while the tea is still hot before adding the ice for better saturation of the sugar) and settle into a comfy chair. I will start with some of the verses that spoke to the fear in my heart. Then I will continue through the progression of that fateful night as we watch my fear turn into strength and courage as I huddled in the darkness with Jesus, my fierce Protector, my *Lion of Juda*.

> *"Be merciful to me, O LORD, for I am in distress; my eyes grow weak with sorrow, my soul and my body with grief."* <u>Psalm 31:9</u> *(NIV)*

> *"For I have heard the slander of many; fear was on every side; while they took counsel together against me, they devised to take away my life."* <u>Psalms 31:13</u> (KJV)

> *"Keep me O LORD, from the hands of the wicked; preserve me from the violent man; who have purposed to overthrow my goings."* <u>Psalm 140:4</u> (KJV)

The violent man... see what I mean? Those scriptures were describing my exact situation. God sees all and He knows all. GOD knew who my enemies were and what my enemy's plans were. What my enemies thought they were doing in the concealment of darkness was revealed just as it is written in Matthew 10:25. There are no secrets that can be hidden in the dark. The light of Jesus shines into the darkest of dark places. GOD even knows the thoughts and plans of the devil, yet the devil does not know the thoughts nor the plans of GOD. Tell me then, who is more powerful and whom will you serve?

> *"Fear them not therefore: for there is nothing covered, that shall not be revealed; and hid, that shall not be known."* <u>Matthew 10:26</u> (KJV)

While reading through the book of Psalms during those three days I began to notice different words and phrases jumping out at me, grabbing my attention. Things that GOD was going to do against those that sought my demise!

> *"Let them be ashamed and confounded together that seek after my soul to destroy it; let them be driven backward and put to shame that wish me evil."* <u>Psalm 40:14</u> (KJV)

I did witness the bewildered and confounded look of confusion upon the faces of those that were plotting against me as to how I knew of their plans and how I escaped. I actually told them how I knew but they did not believe because they do not know Jesus. Their bewildered look brought a smile to my face. Not a smug smile, but a thankful smile from remembering Psalm 40:14.

They thought no one would ever know. But I knew, not of myself, but straight from GOD's Breath to my ears through His Holy Spirit. He warned me of the dangers to my life and protected me even though many times I was unaware of how I knew… I just knew. As this journey progresses I am understanding how GOD talks to me through Holy Spirit. Nonbelievers may find it difficult to understand that what looks impossible in this natural realm is possible for GOD. But this book reveals the truth of Jesus as my Protector and Holy Spirit as my witness. Without Jesus there with me I would not have escaped and there would be no testimony… no me!

As I continued reading the book of Psalms I was becoming confident that GOD had a plan! I certainly could not see a way out, but I had faith that He was in control of the situation. Let me tell you, it was liberating to relinquish my *fix it myself* control and witness His mighty power over my enemies.

> *"Let the wicked fall into their own nets, while I pass by in safety."* <u>Psalm 141:10</u> (NIV)

> *"Let their way be dark and slippery, And let the angel of the LORD pursue them. For without cause they have hidden their net for me in a pit, Which they have dug without cause for my life."* <u>Psalm 35:6-7</u> (NKJV)

Hope came in the written promises of His Word! After all, He had already saved my life so many times before. Like I said before, I could *feel* His Holy presence and I could *hear* His Holy Breath in my ears through His Word. Hope was definitely building; fear was definitely subsiding.

> *"They spread a net for my feet—- I was bowed down in distress. They dug a pit in my path—- but they have fallen into it themselves. Selah"* Psalm 57:6 (NIV)

It did not take long before my eyes began to catch words to give me courage over the fear that had me in its grip. I knew Jesus was fighting for me. After all, He just had them fall into the pit that they had dug for me! Figuratively speaking of course, but there really was a pit involved and I recall that this verse actually made me laugh out loud with joy! I hoped those that may have been lurking outside heard me laugh and wondered in confusion why I was no longer afraid... if they only knew!

Never before in my life had I felt Jesus' presence to be so protective. In the past, He saved me through miracles which I realized after the fact, and sometimes was unaware of altogether. Now however, I was in the middle of His miraculous works with a front-row seat as a witness of Jesus fighting a battle against those that were seeking to take my life. I cannot describe how I felt then nor how I feel now because the experience of His nearness is beyond any words I have in my limited vocabulary. It is truly one of those things one just has to experience for oneself. As I read the following Scriptures I could feel hope building into courage. It was sneaking up on me like a gentle rolling wave on a calm sea.

> *"He delivered me from my strong enemy, and from them which hated me; for they were too strong for me."* Psalm 18:17 (KJV)

> *"You are my hiding place and my shield; I hope in Your word."* Psalm 119:114 (KJV)

GOD is beyond being miraculous. He is supernatural with powers we mere mortals cannot comprehend! Oh how difficult to limit the verses! There are so many that touched my heart and eradicated the gripping paralysis of fear that held me hostage! These Scriptures replaced my fear with His strength. I was beginning to have courageous indignation that was growing stronger with each verse! His Words were becoming embedded into my thoughts and coming through into my spoken words. I even caught myself reading out loud *"Away from me, you evildoers...!"*

> *"Away from me, you evildoers, that I may keep the commands of my GOD!"* <u>Psalm 119-115</u> (NIV)

> *"The LORD is on my side; I will not fear: What can man do to me?"* <u>Psalm 118:6</u> (KJV)

At this point fear was crushed with a mighty title wave of the courage His Word had instilled within my heart! The battle had been won! It was just a matter of time before that particular war was over and, of course, Jesus was victorious! All the glory to Father GOD! Amen!

On the morning of Good Friday, GOD's plan for my escape continued. I had to stay calm on the outside and go through my daily routine as my heart was racing within my chest with anticipation of GOD's next move! My hope for escape was in trusting Jesus completely with my life. I knew without a doubt that He was there making a way where I could see no way just the day before.

By 9:15 a.m. I was in the middle of doing laundry as though nothing had happened when all of a sudden, I had an overwhelming urgency to run for my life! I distinctly heard GOD saying deep within me to *"Flee!"*, but this time with urgency and flee I did! Within three minutes I had grabbed my bible, my journals, my mother's quilt made with her own loving hands, my gun, my purse, the clothes on my back and was pulling out of the driveway!

GOD did not get an argument from me! I did not question, *"Where will I go?"*, *"Flee in what?"*, or "What will I do for money?" I fled as instructed, for my very life was at stake! Thank GOD I was fully dressed and ready to go when He fired His starting gun! Talk about the twinkling of an eye, that is how fast Jesus will appear. But instead of saying, *"Flee!",* Jesus will be saying, *"Come".* Then within the time period of less than a nanosecond I will be with Him forever! Praise GOD!

GOD's Promises to us, His Word, truly is alive and timeless! Praise GOD that He protected me from close calls thwarting the efforts of the evil one's attempts to take my life. And not once did I see a spaceship! (I had to throw that in as it is a throw-back to my previously mentioned book.) All the glory to GOD because most of the time I did not even know I was in danger until after the fact. GOD does not need my help... I need His. I am nothing without Him and can do nothing without Him! I cannot even breathe without Him, literally! I will glorify and praise Him until my last breath!

> *"Great is the LORD, and greatly to be praised; And His greatness is unsearchable."* **Psalm 145:3** (NKJV)

> *"Let everything that has breath praise the LORD. Praise the LORD."* **Psalm 150:6** (NIV)

Reading Psalms was the beginning of discovering the substance of the mysteries of GOD's Living Word. It was the beginning of repentance and restoration of my soul; the beginning of my long journey back into the full radiance of His Light. **I pray that you sit and read the book of Psalms in times of fear and be prepared to be in awe of His majestic and mysterious ways.**

Thank you, Jesus, Lion of the tribe of Juda, my Shepherd, my Savior, my Everything!

> *"The LORD is my shepherd; I shall not want."* **Psalm 23:1** (KJV)

❀ ❀ ❀

"For God may speak in one way, or another, Yet man does not perceive it. In a dream, in a vision of the night, When deep sleep falls upon men, While slumbering on their beds, Then He opens the ears of men, And seals their instruction." <u>Job 33:14-16</u> (NKJV)

❀ ❀ ❀

Chapter 2
Seek The Shepherd's Voice

○ ○ ○

It is a most wonderous miracle to hear my Shepherd's voice through scripture! I have faith that Jesus will be there with me when I stand before Father GOD on the day of judgement. He will not say I have not sinned. No, Jesus, my Sacrificial Lamb, will say I have no sin debts because He paid for all of them with the price of His Life's Blood upon the Cross at Calvary. *Thank You Jesus!*

After reading Psalms, and after I was safely away from the evil that sought to harm me, I began to read my bible faithfully. It was suggested to me to start in Proverbs to get a jump-start, so to speak, on GOD's words of wisdom. I read a chapter a day, month after month for almost a year (Along with other scriptures too, of course). Proverbs is not only full of knowledge from GOD to help guide us through life, but it explains the importance of understanding the wisdom of His Word and of hearing His voice through His Word.

> *"For wisdom will enter your heart, and knowledge will be pleasant to your soul. Discretion will protect you, and understanding will guard you."* <u>Proverbs 2:10-11</u> (NIV)

<u>The Holy Bible</u> is full of many life lessons that can be applied to us today. Even now I notice that there is something pertinent to my day, my situation and so on. It may be the answer to something I have been trying to decide on. It may be the answer to a prayer. It may be an

eye-opening revelation and so on! To my amazement I see mysteries that can explain my yesterdays, guide me through my todays and prepare me for my tomorrows. That is GOD's Living Word! It is the Wisdom of the Breath of GOD's spoken Word as given directly to us on every page. I cannot get enough. I do not want to miss out on anything He has to tell me. If I do the loss is totally mine. You too can have this communication through His word which is how to achieve a personal one-on-one relationship with Jesus.

All the praise and glory to GOD Almighty! Do not leave out one precious word or you could suffer the consequences for lack of understanding, such as I did! I pray that my testimony may spare you from wandering around without guidance and direction; lost in the desert without the Bread of Life, The Living Waters of Jesus Christ, our Savior. I implore you, listen to GOD's warnings about what the devil can do to make your life a living hell through poor choices made without knowledge of His wisdom!

How can one *listen to GOD*? Read and study His Word during quiet time with Him. Then read and study some more. As each day passes, as I read and study and spend time talking with Jesus, I can *hear* Him with more and more clarity. Right now I can hear Jesus telling me the same thing He told the man at the pool at Bethesda in Jerusalem after He healed the man of an infirmity of 38 years…

> *"Afterwards Jesus found him in the temple, and said to him, 'See, you have been made well. Sin no more, lest a worse thing come upon you.'"* **John 5:14** (NKJV)

I hear You loud and clear Jesus! Thank you Jesus! A worse thing did indeed almost happen to me as I could have lost my life but for Your great grace and mercy upon me. I will never stop telling people how You saved my life!

Nanette Crapo

I see myself in many of the stories in Scripture. There are numerous people that I can relate to because their stories and their sins are timeless. We can all benefit from reading, studying, and learning about them. GOD's Word is certainly healing my heart by opening my eyes and I pray they are doing the same for you!

> *"Awake to righteousness, and sin not; for some have not the knowledge of GOD: I speak this to your shame."*
> <u>1 Corinthians 15:34</u> (KJV)

That scripture has meaning to me in that I was guilty of sinning against GOD in my ignorance. I was unaware I was sinning against Him and that is not an excuse, it is a shameful fact. I repented for my sins as I discovered what they were even though I have been beating myself up over them. That too is a sin, not forgiving oneself when Jesus has already paid the price for forgiveness. For this sin I have also repented. I still have so much to learn!

> *"If we confess our sins, He is faithful and just to forgive us our sins and to cleanse us from all unrighteousness."*
> <u>1 John 1:9</u> (NKJV)

Jesus is definitely working on me on our journey together. I had no idea how much would be revealed to me about GOD, Jesus, the Holy Spirit and myself along the way to healing. But it is not just for me. This book is also for anyone that needs healing in spirit, heart and soul.

Very recently, I had a nightmare that turned into a hilarious dream. It must be included in this chapter as it gives further testimony as to one of the many ways GOD talks to me. It also gives testimony as to how far Jesus has brought me since starting this book. I have come a long way in that I now trust Him and turn to Him for everything, big and small, seeking His will for me, and listening for His voice.

"The Dream" Nanette Crapo April 9, 2019

The dream started as a nightmare with an evil creature crawling up the side of my mattress. I could hear the scratching of its claws as it got closer and closer to my right hand that was laying close to the edge of the mattress (as it was in real life). I was paralyzed with fear in my dream just like I had been in real life when the man was creeping up on me in my room when I was 18 years old. Have you ever noticed how the devil and his minions are all about unidentifiable scary noises in the dark? They never jump out at you and yell *"BOO!"* No, they creep and crawl about in the dark to frighten you out of your wits and intimidate you into paralysis.

Anyway, the evil creepy crawler in my dream grabbed my exposed right hand. I tried to call out to Jesus, but it came out in a distorted breathy whisper as my mouth was also paralyzed from fear. It did not matter though, because I was calling for Jesus in my mind. My Shepherd heard me in my time of terror even in my sleep. Just as in real life Jesus responded immediately because He is always with me. He never leaves me as His Spirit is within me!

All of a sudden, I became fierce with the strength of the *Lion of Juda... JESUS*! I grabbed that things creepy withered hand with my left hand and held on with a death grip! I meant business! I was just about to thrash that nasty thing against the nightstand until it was pulverized or vaporized, whichever happened first. I woke myself up slinging my arms around!

I started laughing! My left hand and my right hand were locked together in that *death grip*! (Talk about the left hand not knowing what the right hand is doing...) I laugh again now to remember the dream. The nightmare turned into a glorious revelation from GOD. I know in my heart that GOD was telling me that He will never leave me if I keep hold of His right hand and that He will give me supernatural strength against the terror of the night in the name of Jesus. I do not know about you, but I never again want to be without the peace of GOD's presence. I pray you experience it for yourself. If you do, you too will never let Him go!

> *"Howbeit when He, the Spirit of Truth, is come, He will guide you into all truth: for He shall not speak of Himself; but whatsoever He shall hear that shall He speak, and He will shew you things to come."*
> <u>John 16:13</u> (KJV)

That's Holy Spirit that dwells within the hearts of believers. GOD tells Holy Spirit things that He wants us to know; things that will teach us, guide us, warn us and protect us. What important life's lessons is GOD trying to teach you that you are not hearing? I missed out on forty years' worth! Do not waste such time as I did out of defiant self-will or for whatever reason you think you have. There is no justifiable reason! Call upon Him, listen and you will hear Him!

Now I do not claim to interpret dreams other than those that GOD reveals to me. Many of my own dreams still remain a mystery to me and I have a book full of them. However, I do believe that GOD is telling me not to forget that He is in complete control, He knows my needs, and He protects me so that I am not to fear the things that go "bump" in the night!

Before being enlightened with His Word I was actually in a constant state of confusion as to whether I was following GOD's will or my own. Confusion is but a distraction from the devil.

> *"For GOD is not the author of confusion, but of peace..."*
> <u>1 Corinthians 14:33</u> (KJV)

Confusion was, and is, a dangerous state to be living in. If I am confused and unable to decide about something, about anything for that matter, then I get in a quiet place and pray. When the answer comes peace comes with it. Without this knowledge how then can I distinguish the difference between GOD's Voice, my own thoughts, or the deceitful lies of the *stranger*?

> *"And a stranger will they not follow, but will flee from him; for they know not the voice of strangers."*
> <u>*John 10:9*</u> (KJV)

My point is, I hear my *Shepherd's Voice* through dreams as well as other ways just like scripture says at the beginning of this chapter. (Job 33:14-16) This then is a definite benefit that you may not have considered. You too can *hear* Jesus, the Son of GOD, the Good Shepherd, if you only seek and receive Him into your heart.

> *"And there was a cloud that overshadowed them; and a voice came out of the cloud, saying, 'This is my beloved Son; hear Him.'"* <u>*Mark 9:7*</u> (KJV)

❂ ❂ ❂

"Then spake Jesus again unto them, saying, I Am the Light of the world: he that followeth Me shall not walk in darkness, but shall have the Light of Life." <u>John 8:12</u> (KJV)

❂ ❂ ❂

Chapter 3
Believe The Promises Of God

○ ○ ○

LIGHT LOVE LIFE

This chapter is for everyone that is seeking a very personal one-on-one relationship with Jesus. It is especially for nonbelievers that wish to draw near to the light of Jesus and have GOD'S promise of everlasting life. Jesus will not turn you away if you seek Him.

> *"All that the Father giveth Me shall come to Me; and him that cometh to Me I will in no wise cast out."*
> *John 6:37* (KJV)

Are you ready to meet Jesus? Let me ask you in another way. Will you be horror stricken at the moment of death to find yourself with the dark evil shadow entities like the ones I saw; or will you be smiling in the presence of Jesus like my mother was? (Both discussed in my first book.) GOD has given you a choice! Do not forfeit your free gift of everlasting life for lack of choosing. It is totally your choice whether you accept His love or not. Jesus *is* love and He is patiently waiting for you to accept Him.

> *"Love is patient, love is kind. It does not envy; it does not boast. It is not proud. It does not dishonor others. It is not self-seeking, it is not easily angered, it keeps*

no record of wrongs. Love does not delight in evil but rejoices with the truth. It always protects, always trusts, always hopes, always perseveres. Love never fails."
<u>*1 Corinthians 13:4-8*</u> (NIV)

Jesus loved us to the point of His death, and He loves us still. Nothing can separate us from the love of Jesus, not even death itself for He has given us victory over death and the grave. Now that is not only love, that is true love; agape Jesus kind of love!

Such is Jesus' love that dwells within the hearts of believers as found in the *fruit of the Spirit.* How else does the Holy Spirit change one's heart? In case you have forgotten the fruit of the Spirit found in Galatians, I will list them for you:

love,
faith,
peace,
joy,
gentleness,
goodness,
patience,
meekness, and
temperance.
(Not necessarily in that order.)

Jesus is all of the above. He gives us of Himself, His Holy Spirit, when we have faith and believe in Him! Holy Spirit in turn gives us direct access to Father GOD through Jesus. That completes the Trinity! WOW!

All of a sudden, I understand the Trinity like never before! What a revelation! Is not this the most fantastic journey ever? I had never fully grasp the concept of The Holy Trinity until now! However, now I can clearly see how They Three are One, yet separate! This truly is a journey of learning as well as healing! Radically awesome!

I now have a deeper understanding and appreciation of how the *Light of the World, the Light of Life, Jesus Christ, my Savior, dispels the darkness of depression* in my life on a daily basis. He does it out of His profound love for me! And GOD loves you just as much as He loves me. He does not show favoritism, for we are all His favorite children; therefore, He lavishes His love on us all. It is up to you to accept His only Begotten Son as your Savior and receive His agape kind of love. There is nothing that can compare with it.

> *"And now these three remain: faith, hope and love. But the greatest of these is love." 1 Corinthians 13:13* (NIV)

Remember that GOD's Word is His very Breath and is as good as a Promise for He cannot lie! That is the importance of having knowledge of His Word. I pray that I never again blunder through life of my own accord, listening to the fabricated, twisted, manipulated words of the devil. I thank GOD that He is not a GOD of confusion. Through Jesus as my Savior I have found renewed life for my broken heart, and renewed strength for my soul.

> *"I pray that out of His glorious riches He may strengthen you with power through His Spirit in your inner being..." Ephesians 3:16* (NIV)

GOD has made all, even the master of evil, Satan. Satan can only create havoc and chaotic situations through manipulations and lies. He cannot create life, but he certainly can create death for nonbelievers. It is a death in the hell that was created for him (Satan) and the angels that follow him.

> *"Then shall He say also unto them on the left hand, 'Depart from me, ye cursed, into everlasting fire, prepared for the devil and his angels.'" Matthew 25:41* (KJV)

It is Satan's mission to fill hell with as many souls as he can. In the end times he will have you worshiping him and serving him as slaves in his pit of torment and fire. If you reject Jesus you are also rejecting GOD's gift of eternal life and you are automatically accepting death and hell. Once there it's fun and games over for you and there will be eternal suffering. Do not think that Jesus does not care. He weeps for you, but Father GOD has given you a free will to choose for yourself. So, I strongly urge you to not wait any longer... GOD's stopwatch is ticking. Where will you find yourself when it stops... in a dark tortuous place or in the radiant *Light of Life,* Jesus?

> *"...I am the light of the world: he that followeth me shall not walk in darkness but shall have the Light of Life."* **John 8:12** (KJV)

Or... will you follow Satan and believe his lies that GOD is not real?

> *"The fool says in his heart, 'There is no GOD.' They are corrupt, their deeds are vile; there is no one who does good."* **Psalm 14:1** (NIV)

The devil has no authority over my life unless I relinquish it to him. And as you can see from my testimony, I was unknowingly giving him authority through my ignorance. Do you not see the magnitude of the importance of knowing GOD's Word? Whenever he tries to attack me in the future all I have to do is to *resist him* through the Word of GOD and yell at him with authority, ***"FLEE IN THE NAME OF JESUS!"***

> *"Submit yourselves therefore to GOD. Resist the devil and he will flee from you."* **James 4:7** (KJV)

Wake up, please! If you do not accept Jesus before it is too late, you will be the only one to blame for your eternal suffering! The choice is yours. There is no sitting on the fence in this life or death decision! GOD cannot make it any clearer that if you do not believe Jesus is the Son of GOD you are condemning yourself for your decision is in your control!

> *"... but he that believeth not is condemned already, because he hast not believed in the name of the only Begotten Son of GOD." John 3:18* (KJV)

After reading this book, you cannot say, "I didn't know I just didn't know..." There are no excuses that GOD has not heard. GOD knows what you know, and He knows what's in your heart. You cannot lie nor hide from GOD! Once in hell, Jesus cannot help you and you cannot hide from Satan! You think you are depressed now? Magnify your depression a million thousand times and you may come close to the depth of depression and anguish you will suffer eternally if you are putting your trust in the devil's lies.

I can do nothing without Jesus. I understand nothing unless He opens my mind with knowledge of the wisdom of His Word. I cannot *see* Him in His Word unless He opens my spiritual eyes. I cannot *hear* Him unless He opens my spiritual ears. He does just that if one seeks Him. He opens eyes and ears so that one *sees* Him in His Word, and *hears* Him through His Word. It's all about reading, learning and talking with Him until His Word is in your heart. That is how one can develop a personal relationship with Jesus, gradually or all of a sudden. You will realize He is right there with you and has been all the time.

> *"But if we walk in the light, as He is in the light, we have fellowship with one another, and the blood of Jesus, His Son, purifies us from all sin." 1 John 1:7* (NIV)

Jesus loves us so much that He allowed Himself to be nailed to the Cross in our place. Do you have faith enough to believe the promises of GOD Almighty?

> *"...having canceled the charge of our legal indebtedness, which stood against us and condemned us, He has taken it away, nailing it to the cross."* **Colossians 2:14** (NIV)

You can receive GOD's gift of eternal life because Jesus has already paid the monumental price of death, hell, and the grave for you, for me, and for the whole world. And please do not let the devil tell you that you are unworthy. None of us are worthy to enter the kingdom of heaven. The only One worthy is our Redeemer, the Lamb of GOD, Jesus Christ. It does not matter who you are or what you have done, Jesus will not turn you away. His phenomenal, incomprehensible love is beyond belief and will simply blow you away if you will only ask Him into your heart as your LORD and Savior. Jesus is waiting with arms open wide... waiting with untold mercy and love. We all need Jesus. We all need to grab hold of His right hand and believe by faith that **HE IS**. Believe, just believe in what is not seen.

> *"But the scripture hath concluded all under sin, that the promise by faith of Jesus Christ might be given to them that believe."* **Galatians 3:22** (KJV)

Please forgive me for going over and over certain points. I realize I have done so, but I feel deeply within my heart that it is a necessity that I do so. Sometimes things do not sink in the first or second time. And for some of us (like myself) it takes several times of hearing the same thing before it hits us with understanding. Things like scriptures I have heard all my life and I just now realize the deep meanings hidden within. So, I will urge you again to lay the burden of your sins at the feet of Jesus if you have not already done so! Find your faith in Jesus Christ at the Cross! He is calling you with His Light, His Love and His very Life! If you have never received Christ as your Savior and you want to answer His call on your heart, you can do so right now. There is a prayer at the end of this book located just prior to the Epilogue that you can pray as you give your life to Jesus. He will change your life forever. His love will not fail you.

Nanette Crapo 03/25/2019

"For I am persuaded that neither death nor life, nor angels nor principalities nor powers, nor things present nor things to come, nor height nor depth, nor any other created thing, shall be able to separate us from the love of GOD which is in Christ Jesus our Lord." **Romans 8:38-39** *(NKJV)*

◦ ◦ ◦

"And ye shall seek me, and find me, when ye shall search for me with all your heart." Jeremiah 29:13 (KJV)

◦ ◦ ◦

Chapter 4

Find The Lamb Of God

○ ○ ○

Nonbelievers that have not accepted Jesus will not have the benefit of having their sin debt erased. It is the only way to eternal life. Through His selfless act of agape (love expressed) at the Cross, Jesus freed us from the law of sin and death.

> *"For the wages of sin is death; but the gift of GOD is eternal life through Jesus Christ our LORD."*
> *Romans 6:23* (KJV)

> *"For the law of the Spirit of life in Jesus Christ hath made me free from the law of sin and death."*
> *Romans 8:2* (KJV)

There it is... GOD's promises are irrevocable. Your salvation, your gift of eternal life in His glorious presence, is a free gift to you but it cost Jesus everything. What a shame to reject this beautiful gift of life that cost Him His Life.

Once you *ask* Jesus into your heart you cannot stop there. *Seek* Him and draw near to Him and *believe* in His Promises. *Find* the Lamb of GOD and surrender your old man self to Him. It is up to you for He will not force His will upon you. **Trust** Him with the faith of a child and He will set you free.

The above is not necessarily the sequence of how the events of salvation are supposed to occur. Heavens no! One can seek Him which leads to believing and accepting. One can have a Damascus moment out of the blue and believe and accept all at once. It is an individual miracle between you and Jesus Christ as your Savior. I am just relaying the sequence of events as to how they happened to me. I had asked Jesus into my heart at age 15 then rested in His love for 50 years... in ignorance. I knew Him, but I really did not know anything about the mysteries of Him. I certainly did not know about the many iniquities of my life that can be found in His Word.

I did not know that there was so much more to learn and understand! I knew nothing of such things as self-will, idolatry, hidden pride (hidden from me, but not from GOD), and spiritual warfare. It is my sincere prayer that my testimony reach others and hopefully prevent endless and unnecessary years of just existing in a depressed and desolate place of backsliding, of wrong believing or of unbelieving. There is hope for us in the Lamb of GOD. When we receive His Spirit we are changed with His agape.

> *"Hereby know we that we dwell in Him, and He in us, because He hath given us of His Spirit."*
> *1 John 4:13* (KJV)

Holy Spirit is GOD's Spirit, the Spirit of Jesus Christ, which is given to all believers by faith.

> *"That Christ may dwell in your hearts by faith;"*
> *Ephesians 3:17* (KJV)

Are you prepared to be awed by Jesus Christ? I can tell you what you can expect when you invite Jesus into your heart. Expect profound love like you have never known! How can this be? It is because Jesus' love is different from your run of the mill "I Love You" kind of love. Jesus' love is truly unconditional and beyond understanding. It is a rare and special kind of love that is deeply passionate. It does not matter what your sins are, where you came from or what you have done. Jesus loves you and will make your heart brand new with His love. *Jesus demonstrated His love for you when He carried your cross, died in your place, and paid your sin debt!* That is the epitome of the agape (love) that Jesus has for you, for me and for the whole world!

The alternative is to continue in misery. You know what I'm talking about; the misery of loneliness, helplessness, and hopelessness. The absolute misery of despair and depression. I know, because that is what I am leaving behind on my journey with Jesus through this book. The more I research, the more I learn, the more I know His love! I pray you come along and stick with me until we reach the end of this journey of healing and discovery with Jesus. It has, thus far, definitely been of great benefit for me and I pray it has for you as well.

The more I study, the more I rely upon the peace of Jesus. I have learned to *be still* and concentrate on Him until He alleviates my feelings of loneliness, sadness, fear, anxiety, depression or whatever the affliction. During this quiet time with Him, my distress melts away. I sit quietly and praise Him with thanksgiving for all the wonders He has done for my family and me throughout my lifetime. As this journey progresses, my down times are lessening, and my joy is increasing. He can and will do the same for you. *Your life will be forever blessed through Jesus Christ and what He did for you at the Cross!*

Have you been missing out on the wonders of all that GOD has for you? I pray you have not. And I pray for the lost souls of nonbelievers that the scales of disbelief be removed from their eyes that they may know the agape of Jesus Christ. My heart bleeds for those such as myself that may be fumbling around in the darkness for lack of knowledge. It does not matter which group you are in. Seize the moment, for Jesus is returning soon! Repent, seek forgiveness, forgive others and seek the Lamb of GOD. He will give you a new heart full of love and teach you how to love not only one another but how to forgive and love yourself and those that have hurt you. Indeed, we are to forgive because He has forgiven us! The devil does not want you to forgive those that hurt you because Jesus told us to forgive as our Heavenly Father has forgiven us. The devil's lies are all about having you believe and do the opposite of what GOD's Word teaches believers to do.

> *"Then Peter came to Jesus and asked, 'LORD, how many times shall I forgive my brother or sister who sins against me: Up to seven times?'" Matthew 18:21* (NIV)

> *"Jesus said to him, 'I do not say to you, up to seven times, but up to seventy times seven."* Matthew 18:22* (NKJV)

I did the math and that would be 490 times. In other words, do not keep track! Forgive and keep forgiving as Heavenly Father forgives you! My own seemingly endless cycle of brokenness could have been much shorter if I had been able to forgive myself as readily as I forgave others. I blamed myself for not being good enough which kept me in bondage to my sins of the past. That in turn prevented me from letting go and moving on.

> *"For if you forgive men their trespasses, your heavenly Father will also forgive you: But if you do not forgive men their trespasses, neither will your Father forgive your trespasses." Matthew 6:14-15* (NKJV)

Ignorance is not a valid excuse. I was holding on to the hurt and the pain of rejection that was born out of my self-depravation and self-condemnation of thinking I did not deserve anything better. I was so sure if I had only loved a little more or given a little more that I would not have been betrayed and rejected. All false accusations from the devil to trap me in his snare of blame and shame for being a failure. Living in the past of *what if's* and dwelling upon my mistakes made it impossible for me to move past the emotional pain.

Another trap of the devil... blame ourselves and wallow in self-pity with the what if's until you go completely insane! That changes absolutely nothing! Is it any wonder why there are so many people on medication for anxiety and depression? I've been there and done that too! But Jesus has paid our sin debt in full and says we are to forgive not only one another, but ourselves as well! That's right! Believers have been cleansed by the Blood of the Sacrificial Lamb of GOD, Jesus Christ. Of what authority do we still condemn ourselves?

Who am I to withhold forgiveness for others or myself? That too, as I am learning, is a sin against GOD. I was refusing the forgiveness of my own sins which Jesus paid so dearly for! So, I am now learning how to let go of the past and move forward into my future! The answer lies in giving it to the Lamb of GOD! Thank you, Jesus, for Your agape and for all You suffered for us!

> *"If we confess our sins, He is faithful and just to forgive us our sins, and to cleanse us from all unrighteousness."*
> *1 John 1:9* (KJV)

Once you confess your sins your heart will be opened to the love and healing that Jesus has for you. Those that have hurt you will no longer do so through your memories. Pray for them. The devil has blinded them and hardened their hearts. Have pity upon their souls. These lost souls are dancing to the strings that the devil himself is pulling! Jesus is the only One that can sever those strings, those bonds, enabling one to escape the clutches of the devil and hades. One of the last things Jesus did upon the cross as our Sacrificial Lamb was to ask Father GOD to forgive us!

> *"Jesus said, 'Father, forgive them, for they do not know what they are doing.'"* *Luke 23:34* (NIV)

I Pray for others that they may be saved by the redeeming Blood of Jesus Christ from eternal suffering in hell. That is a fate worse than death itself! As for me, I choose to keep moving forward on this journey with Jesus, forward toward heaven and life eternal.

> *"...how much more shall the blood of Christ, who through the eternal Spirit offered Himself without spot to God, cleanse your conscience from dead works to serve the living God?" Hebrews 9:14* (NKJV)

> *"For this is my blood of the new testament which is shed for many for the remission of sins." Matthew 26:28* (KJV)

I pray that spiritual eyes are being opened to the truth and purpose of the Blood of the Lamb, Jesus. It is my prayer that all who read this realize that His precious Blood was shed for them. Jesus covers all of our sin debt with His precious Blood which includes us in the promise of Inheritance to GOD's Kingdom. Jesus loves us no matter what! He is my Redeemer, my LORD, my Savior, my Healer, my Friend, my Anchor, my Hope, and so much more! Jesus is my Everything!

Nanette Crapo, December 1, 2019

> *"This hope we have as an anchor of the soul, both sure and steadfast, and which enters the Presence behind the veil," Hebrews 6:19* (NKJV)

> *"This is love: not that we loved God, but that He loved us and sent His Son as an atoning sacrifice for our sins." 1 John 4:10* (NIV)

❖ ❖ ❖

"who Himself bore our sins in His own body on the tree, that we, having died to sins, might live for righteousness—-by whose stripes you were healed."
<u>*1 Peter 2:24*</u> (NKJV)

❖ ❖ ❖

Chapter 5

Trust The Finished Works Of Christ

◦ ◦ ◦

GOD gave all power and dominion to Jesus. Satan will lie to you that he has dominion because of the sins of Adam. Well that curse has been broken by the finished works of Jesus upon the Cross! Satan only has dominion over you if you give it to him! Satan can manipulate you into giving the authority and dominion that you have through Jesus Christ over to him. Satan even tried to trick Jesus into bowing down and worshiping him by taking GOD's Word and manipulating it to suit himself. But Jesus resisted temptation.

> *"Then Jesus said to him, 'Away with you, Satan! For it is written, 'You shall worship the LORD your God, and Him only you shall serve.'" <u>Matthew 4:10</u>* (NKJV)

Satan was no match for Jesus because Jesus knew the Truth of the Word of GOD. *Jesus Is the Word of GOD!*

> *"In the beginning was the Word, and the Word was with God, and the Word was God." <u>John 1:1</u>* (NKJV)

> *"And the Word became flesh and dwelt among us, and we beheld His glory, the glory as of the only begotten of the Father, full of grace and truth."* **John 1:14** (NKJV)

Remember how I have told you that the devil tricked me into believing I was doing GOD's will and pleasing GOD while in truth I was sinning through wrong believing? Trust me, Satan can and will trick you through manipulation of GOD's Word, through out and out lies, through intimidation, and through fear of loneliness and rejection! Do not let that happen... be educated... seek the truth for yourself!

To give in to the fear that the devil tries to put upon you is to tell GOD that you do not trust that He is in complete control! I did not know that until the following miracle happened to me in a moment of fear. The devil had me in the grip of fear as recently as February 2018. Had it not been for my sister, Sharon, standing firm on the healing Promises of GOD's Word, I would have succumbed to Satan's evil plans and no doubt I would have hemorrhaged to death! All the glory to Father GOD and the healing power of Jesus, Yeshua, our Savior!
Nanette Crapo, April 9, 2019

We have already covered that when you seek and find the Lamb of GOD the same power and authority given to Him has been given to you in His Holy Name. That includes, but is not limited to, healing by His stripes. Jesus bore our infirmities including our addictions and afflictions. He nailed them all to the Cross along with our iniquities (sins); which are evident in His scars. We have only to believe by faith and call upon the Name above all names... Jesus.

> *"You came near when I called you, and you said, 'do not fear'. O LORD, you took up my case; you redeemed my life."* **Lamentations 3:57** (NIV)

This testimony is yet another miracle of evidence of the healing hand of Jesus upon me. I literally felt His warm healing touch! Yes, I felt His touch, so say what you will but I will not be swayed! I know He is real and that He is with me always, even in the hospital.

This time I was the patient and I was bleeding internally. I had a feeling of imminent death as my blood count dropped from 10 to 7.8 in a matter of hours with no sigh of letting up. My blood pressure had become dangerously low. My life's blood was flowing out of me into a drainage tube. That was the first time, and I pray the last time, that a garden hose is shoved up my nose!

My sister was about to call my boys to let them know of my situation. A second surgery was being discussed. I felt I had fallen through the cracks and my time on earth was running out. My fear was that I would pass from this earth before I could see my children once more. I wanted to tell them not to be sad for me but to rejoice that we would see each other again one day in heaven. I wanted to pass to my sons that death is not to be feared just as my mother had passed to me so very long ago. I wanted to pass to the next generation my Grandfather's and my Mother's legacy of love and faith for Jesus Christ. Since my ordeal, I have not wasted the chance to do just that!

At that particular time, I truly began to believe that I would be seeing Jesus very soon because His powerful presence had become so very palpable to me. I mentioned this very thing to my sister. It is hard to explain but the very air in the room definitely had a different "feel" about it. Perhaps the atmosphere was saturated with GOD's angels? Perhaps, I cannot prove it, but in my heart I believe it.

My sister reminded me to trust that GOD knew what was happening and He was in complete control. She reminded me of all that God brought me through, and she said to me, *"God did not save you all those times to let you die now."* At the exact moment I acknowledged that she was right, my cell phone rang. A prayer warrior from my church called to check on me as she had missed seeing me Sunday. She did not know I was in the hospital. Only my sister and brother knew at the time.

I briefly told her my situation and she prayed for my healing. During that prayer I felt a light pressure with warmth over the area of my abdomen where the internal bleeding was occurring and where my pain was. I felt the pressure while my eyes were closed during her prayer and thought to myself that it must be the nurses call light / tv remote control that had all of a sudden come to my attention. In addition to praying for my healing by the stripes of Jesus (Isaiah 53:5), she prayed the following scripture over me:

> *"What do you conspire Against the LORD? He will make an utter end of it. Affliction will not rise up a second time." Nahum 1:9* (NKJV)

The latter scripture was a prayer that my affliction would not return! I did not think more about the pressure on my abdomen until after her prayers ended. But I soon discovered that it was a supernatural pressure as there was nothing there in the natural! The call light was between the siderails and the mattress! The warmth was supernatural as well; it was freezing in that hospital room!

That prayer brought forth another miracle and healing that the physicians could not do without performing surgery. My personal physician, Jesus Christ, stopped the bleeding and healed me without surgery. All the glory to GOD! Thank You Heavenly Father. Thank you, Jesus, for Your suffering and for Your stripes that healed me over 2,000 years ago! All the glory to GOD!

> *"But He was wounded for our transgressions, He was bruised for our iniquities; the chastisement of our peace was upon Him; and with His stripes we are healed." Isaiah 53:5* (KJV)

My inner peace was renewed through trusting Jesus, the One that paid dearly for my healing with His stripes and His Life's Blood. The gift of my healing came with a price of such magnitude that I cannot even comprehend it! But, my Savior, Jesus Christ, paid it in full! Thank you Heavenly Father, for Jesus. Thank you Jesus for carrying my Cross with agape, with such Passion.

Nanette Crapo April 9, 2019

> *"I am the living bread that came down from heaven. If anyone eats of this bread, he will live forever. This bread is my flesh, which I will give for the life of the world." **John 6:51** (NIV)*

My fears were alleviated just moments after the above miracles occurred, i.e.:

- the prayer warriors phone call,
- the touch of His healing hand, and
- the sudden change in the drainage tube indicating that bleeding had stopped.

Then as if on cue the hospital chaplain entered my room. I had requested to see him the day before at the time of my admission to the hospital. I wanted to ask him to pray for my healing. He was delighted to hear my testimony of what had just transpired. So, instead of a prayer of healing, I asked him for a prayer of thanksgiving! All the glory to Father GOD in the name of Jesus Christ!

> *"But when Jesus heard it, He answered him, saying 'Fear not: believe only, and she shall be made whole.'" **Luke 8:50** (KJV)*

Since my total surrender in complete brokenness on the night of my *Damascus moment*, Jesus has continued to rescue me. I say "continued" because He has been rescuing me since my infancy! He will do the same for you, no matter what you need, no matter what you have done! He already knows everything you have done anyway as nothing is hidden from Him. He knows what you need before you even ask. So, repent of your sins as I have and lean on Him and there will be no more shame nor condemnation. He will forgive you before your words reach your lips because He knows your heart!

I believe and declare the following verse to be true for me, in the name of Jesus:

> **"I shall not die but live and declare the works of the LORD."** *Psalm 118:17* (KJV)

SECTION 4
Healing Hearts
◦ ◦ ◦

"*Thou hast ravished my heart...*"
<u>*Song of Solomon 4:9*</u> (KJV)

"*I would have lost heart, unless I had believed That I would see the goodness of the LORD In the land of the living.*" <u>*Psalm 27:13*</u> (NKJV)

❋ ❋ ❋

"All we like sheep have gone astray; We have turned, every one, to his own way; And the LORD has laid on Him the iniquity of us all." Isaiah 53:6 (NKJV)

❋ ❋ ❋

CHAPTER 1

Jesus Knows

...

> *"The spirit of a man will sustain him in sickness, But who can bear a broken spirit?"* **Proverbs 18:14** (NKJV)

I know that I am nothing, just a speck of dust in the grand scheme of things. I thank GOD daily for His love and protection for my family and myself. I thank GOD for sending Jesus to save my soul by paying my sin debt. Yet, for all His love and my new-found personal relationship with Jesus, I was still broken. Please let me add here that I was still in my infancy in His Word. I was feeding on the milk of babes to eradicate my ignorance of the mysteries of Jesus Christ.

> *"... as newborn babes, desire the pure milk of the word, that you may grow thereby, if indeed you have tasted that the Lord is gracious."* **1 Peter 2:2** (NKJV)

I had indeed tasted the graciousness of the LORD on an untold number of occasions and I was learning to turn to Him for everything! So, in abject loneliness and brokenness from a lifetime of betrayal and in profound depression and self-isolation from a lifetime of rejection, I prayed through tears from the depth of my soul to me made whole again...

ABBA, Father GOD, I praise You, I worship You and I need You, for I am nothing without You. I thank You for Your great love and mercy as I come before You in the name of Your precious Son, Jesus Christ. I need You Father GOD, for the burden of my tortured soul that I can no longer bear. I am tired from a lifetime of being depressed and living in the past. Please help me to move past all of this rejection and depression Heavenly Father. Please put the shattered pieces of my heart, my spirit and my soul back together for I know that Jesus has already paid the price for my complete healing.

Thank You Father GOD! Thank You for loving me so much that You sent your Only Beloved Son, Jesus Christ to save me! Thank You for loving a sinner such as myself.

Thank You Jesus, for loving me so much that You willingly lay down Your life for mine! In Jesus precious name I pray. Amen.

It was then that I heard God say, "Write a book." Not out loud, but deep within my soul.

Nanette Crapo, November 2018

Then in January 2019 while watching my favorite Christian channel, a pastor looked right out of the t.v. at me and said that GOD told him to tell me to "Write that book!"... so I started writing "a book" which became two books. Thank you Pastor Grey for your well timed words of encouragement! (I told you GOD can speak through other people, even people on television.)

> **"I said, LORD, be merciful unto me; heal my soul; for I have sinned against thee." Psalm 41:4** (KJV)

GOD has answered my prayer and He has done so very much more! GOD in His mercy has blessed me with two books out of that one. This is the second of these first two books. He has already given me more subjects for future books as I learn and heal on this current journey with Jesus.

GOD *is* an awesome GOD indeed. He knows our hearts. There are no secrets He does not already know. Take everything to Him in prayer and it will change your life for there is nothing He cannot do! Nothing is impossible for GOD!

> *"Restore unto me the joy of my salvation; and uphold me with thy free Spirit." Psalm 51:12* (KJV)

Our scars may be from the same kind of wounds, but the testimonies behind those scars are as individual and unique as we are. *Jesus has sympathy and empathy of our suffering and anguish. He gives testimony as to His unconditional love for us in His scars!* What do your scars have to tell the world? What is your testimony?

The rest of this chapter is for all that have suffered isolation, rejection and depression due to feelings of being unwanted or unloved. I bet that pretty much covers nearly everyone! The following is for everyone that has ever been hated without a cause, for Jesus knows of such things as that too! The following is for everyone whose heart is so compassionate and loving that it is impossible to comprehend the cold and calculating hearts that are void of love. The following is for everyone that, sadly, has never experienced the fruit of the Spirit of the love of Jesus at all and cannot understand those that have! The following is for all that are seeking forgiveness, acceptance, truth and most of all... love.

Jesus knows and understands every kind of agony and despair known to man. He can fill your heart with His agape kind of love that is beyond understanding; changing your life forever if you will just trust in Him! **Jesus knows because there is nothing you have suffered that He has not suffered 10x10, 10x10, and ten times ten more! It is beyond comprehension how much He suffered for us!**

My testimony is not to seek your sympathy nor your pity. I have had enough feelings of self-pity to cover millions of people. It is my prayer, my mission, to tell you how much more Jesus knows the heartbreak of rejection, and the loneliness of depression. All one has to do is read The

<u>Holy Bible.</u> Jesus suffered beyond anything that anyone can fathom! That is how He has empathy in addition to His sympathy for us.

He understands everything we are feeling and going through because He identifies with it on a personal level deep within His very soul! His compassion and love for us knows no bounds. Jesus loves us with such a profound passion that He suffered for us what no man has suffered before or since!

Jesus took all our sins upon His sinless body as He suffered death and hell in our place. No one, and I truly mean no one, has ever done that! No one but Jesus has ever been worthy; without spot, without blemish, and without sin. Only the blood of Jesus, the Lamb of GOD qualifies! Without Jesus, the Only Begotten Son of GOD, we would all be lost and without hope!

Jesus has been there and done that out of His love for Father GOD, for you and for me. *There is no greater love than the love of Jesus. Jesus is Agape!*

> *"Greater love has no man than this, than to lay down one's life for his friends."* <u>**John 15:13**</u> (NKJV)

Jesus is the answer to everything! Put your faith in Him!
<u>**I am begging all of you out there that suffer the affliction of depression for whatever the cause. Do not fall into the devil's dark pit! Do not hold it within yourself as you know full well by now that you can do nothing by yourself! Please seek professional help and seek Jesus!**</u>

There is a way out of the downward spiral. I am living proof! There is a way to "just let go" and to "move on" and that way has a name... Jesus! He will lift you up with His love! He is already right there with you, waiting for you to acknowledge Him and accept Him into your heart! Your life is a blessing from GOD and worth living with Jesus in your heart!

> *"He heals the brokenhearted and binds up their wounds."* <u>**Psalm 147:3**</u> (NIV)

Agape is the kind of passionate and unconditional love that is backed up with actions. It goes beyond mere words. It is the kind of love my mother displayed. Though she lacked the words expressing her love for her children and others, she expressed it in her selfless and tireless actions. As an adult I can look back and totally identify. Jesus has that kind of passionate love for all of us even while we are yet sinners. Make no mistake, He sees us as we really are, yet he loves us anyway.

Jesus has freed me from the bondage of the curse of desire for my mate. My desire is for Jesus Christ. My desire is to love and please Him. My desire is to keep His love for me guarded within my heart. It is reasonable to desire your husband's love, but your first desire should always be the desire for Jesus' love and to return that love to Him as your Lord and Savior!

> *"Keep your heart with all diligence, For out of it spring the issues of life." Proverbs 4:23* (NKJV)

Love is a gift and not a prize to be earned or bought. GOD's love for us is evident in His plan of salvation. Jesus' love for us is evident in that He lay down His life in exchange for ours. That act of agape purchased eternal life for all that believe.

> *"Keep yourselves in GOD's love as you wait for the mercy of our LORD Jesus Christ to bring you to eternal life." Jude 8:21* (NIV)

Just to think about how I have hurt Jesus after all He sacrificed for me out of His pure and faithful agape truly wounds me deeply. I now realize how I have betrayed Him just as I have been betrayed! Through scripture GOD has opened my eyes as to my own selfish ways, albeit in the name of love.

How terrible and unjust of me to whine when Jesus' pain, agony, and depression far surpasses anything I have suffered and far surpasses anything my mind can imagine! I pass along to you that *Jesus knows*. I pray this book helps those of you that may be trapped in the ruts of your own tracks from years and years of circling around in your own private hell, whatever that hell may be. *Jesus knows exactly what you are suffering. It bears repeating, there is nothing known to man that Jesus did not suffer. Keep in mind that He suffered for you and for me.*

Now I ask you to use your imagination. Draw upon your memories of all you have suffered and multiply it all by, let's say… hundreds of thousands of millions. (If that is possible. I never was very strong in math.) My point is that you still would not come close to being able to fathom the depth of the suffering that He endured out of His equally unfathomable and unconditional agape for us. GOD's plan of salvation to save us sinners would not have happened if Jesus had not loved us! It is beyond my intellectual capacity to understand how He can love me like that!

> ***"But GOD, who is rich in mercy, for His great love wherewith He loved us." Ephesians 2:4*** (KJV)

> ***"Behold, a virgin shall be with child, and bring forth a son, and they shall call His name Emmanuel, which being interpreted is, God with us." Matthew 1:23*** (KJV)

He came to be our Savior (Jesus, *Yeshua*). *So, can you see that nothing exists to compare to what Jesus suffered as He hung upon the Cross in our place to give us* eternal Life… nothing!

> ***"Wanting to satisfy the crowd, Pilate released Barabbas to them. He had Jesus flogged, and handed him over to be crucified. Mark 15:15*** (NIV)

Talk about a broken heart and a crushed spirit! Only Father GOD and Jesus Himself knows how much pain and suffering He endured. He was betrayed and rejected by those that He loved, crushing His very Spirit. Even after death, His side was pierced to make sure He was dead. I cannot even begin to imagine what Jesus experienced when taking the dark sins of the world upon or into Himself. It might possibly have been the worst part of His torture!

> *"And when the sixth hour was come, there was darkness over the whole land until the ninth hour."* <u>Mark 15:33</u> (KJV)

Jesus knows the feeling of utter isolation and depression. After He took the darkness of the sins of the whole world upon Himself, *He cried out in His agony and His loneliness of being separated from Father GOD*:

> *"E-lo'-I, E-lo'-I, la'-ma sa-bach'-tha-ni? which is, being interpreted, 'My GOD, My GOD, why hast thou forsaken me'?"* <u>Mark 15:34</u> (KJV)

GOD cannot look upon sin therefore, for the first and last time ever Jesus was separated from His Heavenly Father.

> *"Hide thy face from my sins, and blot out all mine iniquities."* <u>Psalm 51:9</u> (KJV)

When Jesus took the sins of the world upon Himself as our Sacrificial Lamb, the veil of the holy temple was torn. This veil was a barrier between the people and GOD. It was the Holy of Holy places, the inner sanctuary. The only person allowed to enter behind the veil was the anointed high priest who entered on behalf of the people. There was no guarantee that the priest would come back out alive, so he entered with a rope tied around his waist in case he died, for whatever reason, behind the veil. If he did indeed die, he could be pulled out by the rope.

Anyone else that entered behind the veil without being anointed by GOD would die instantly. Jesus removed the need for the veil, giving us direct access to Father GOD. Jesus is our High Priest. He is the 50th and the last High Priest, and He shall remain so forever.

> *"Then the veil of the temple was torn in two from top to bottom. So when the centurion, who stood opposite Him, saw that He cried out like this and breathed His last, he said, 'Truly this Man was the Son of GOD'!"* Mark 15:38-39 (NKJV)

When you accept Jesus as your LORD and Savior, your sins will be erased, and your name will be written by Jesus Himself in the Lambs Book of Life. Once He has written your name in His Book, it cannot be blotted out. What are you waiting for? He has already paid the price for you.

Jesus knows what it really means to sacrifice oneself for another. He knew that what He was to bear (the "cup") was going to be beyond anything that can even be put into words.

> *"...O my FATHER, if it be possible, let this cup pass from me: nevertheless, not as I will, but as thou wilt."* Matthew 26:39 (KJV)

Jesus knows the agony of monumental anxiety in His soul, right up until His horrific death! Jesus was in such distress and agony for what was to come that *He sweat blood!*

> *"And being in an anguish, He prayed more earnestly, and His sweat was like drops of blood falling to the ground."* Luke 22:44 (NIV)

Jesus knows the depths of depression that one can reach...

> *"My soul is exceeding sorrowful, even unto death:"* Matthew 26:38 (KJV)

Jesus knows rejection and being hated unjustly by those He loved...

"'They hated me without reason." John 15:25 (NIV)

I pray that you remember that Jesus suffered in our place and in doing so He spared us from having to endure the same! So, the next time you want to throw a pity party, fall to your knees and call on Jesus instead. He feels your pain. He will comfort you. He will deliver you from (fill in the blank with *whatever you need Him to deliver you* from), i.e.: addiction, illness, loneliness, depression, anxiety, etc. Nothing is to large nor too small for Him because He loves you.

Jesus gave His very flesh for the life of the world... for you and me! He was scourged and beaten until His flesh was gone from off His bones! I will never forget what my salvation cost Jesus, Yeshua, my Savior. I pray that no matter what you are suffering or what your burden is, that you always remember... ***JESUS KNOWS!***

> *"Seeing then that we have a great High Priest who has passed into the heavens, Jesus the Son of GOD, let us hold fast our confession."*
>
> *"For we do not have a High Priest who cannot sympathize with our weaknesses; but with all points tempted as we are, yet without sin."* **Hebrews 4:14-15** (NKJV)

◦ ◦ ◦

"To know the love of Christ which passes knowledge; that you may be filled with all the fulness of GOD."
<u>*Ephesians 3:19*</u> *(NKJV)*

◦ ◦ ◦

CHAPTER 2

Agape
The Love Letter
April 10, 2019

◦ ◦ ◦

It is tremendously difficult for me to divulge the following revelation. It is extremely personal and until now very private. It has to do with my emotional and mental state of depression that almost ended my life. It has to do with my selfishness, my pity parties for "suffering" heartache and loneliness. And as shameful as it is to tell you this, I must… I took His love for granted! I became too familiar with His presence and His love.

It has to do with my incessant whining to GOD about my "brokenness". But if it will save even one life from suicidal thoughts of despair while in the pit of depression because of the lies of Satan, it will be worth baring my soul for all to see.

I pray you read the following very carefully and read it often so that understanding may be written upon your heart as it has been written upon mine.

Just a note here: ***I have been whining, crying, and begging for a soul mate and all the while I have been calling Jesus my Everything…***

The following scriptures are some that began to grab my attention as understanding of His love began to sink into my bones.

> *"Even so ye also outwardly appear righteous unto men, but within ye are full of hypocrisy and iniquity."* <u>Matthew 23:28</u> (KJV)
>
> *"Ye blind guides, which strain at a gnat, and swallow a camel."* <u>Matthew 23:24</u> (KJV)
>
> *"Nevertheless I have this against you, that you have left your first love."* <u>Revelation 2:4</u> (NKJV)

All of a sudden the following words came into my heart like a lightning bolt! They are from Jesus to my heart through His Holy Spirit that dwells within me! It is very clear to me that I am to share them with the world! I call His words "***The Love Letter***". I pray that they penetrate deep within your heart and sear your very soul as they have mine!

'Really? Your Everything?'

Why do you cry for those that can give you nothing of what you seek or need?
Why do you cry for love lost that was nothing but lies and trickery from the beginning?
Why do you cry for waiting so long for your true soul mate?
Why do you cry for your broken heart and shattered soul?

<u>What do you know of such things?</u>

Have you suffered the betrayal and rejection of thousands upon thousands and thousands more?
Have you stood faithfully outside the doorway of time itself, knocking; waiting patiently throughout eternity for hearts to open to you?
Have you suffered physically the torment and agony of being scourged, willingly taking the burden of the sins of the world upon your broken body; then willingly being crucified upon the Cross by the very ones whose sin debt you paid for with your own life's blood?

What do you know of betrayal and rejection?
What do you know of a broken heart and a shattered soul?

Is not My love enough for you?
Is not My heart enough for you?
Is not My shed blood, My life, enough for you?
How much more of everything do you need from Me before you stop crying for your lost love?

I Am He that stands before you daily...
I Am He that loves you unconditionally and for evermore...
There Is No Other!'

WOW!!! I am at my local library, typing as fast as these thoughts have come into my heart. I sit here crying for the Passion in His Words. I am at a loss for words right now...

> "The LORD has chastened me severely, But He has not given me over unto death." **Psalm 118:18** (NKJV)

I cannot read the above without crying with a mixture of shame for taking His love for granted and of glorious awe for the depth of His Passion that has saturated my heart! I never want to forget His Words to me, to us! They have been engraved upon my very soul! Jesus is Agape... pure breathtakingly blinding love the likes of which I have never experienced from another and never will! The love I craved from man is nothing compared to the love I now embrace from Jesus! His Love permeates my very soul! His love will not fade away from me; it will not betray me; it will not judge me; and it will not be taken from me! His love is mine forever and my love is His forever! Forgive me Jesus, for being so blind! I love You Jesus!
Nanette Crapo, April 10, 2019

Jesus has chastised me with His profound love that what I have been seeking all my life is already mine. Jesus Christ is my Heart, my Love, my

Soul, my Soul Mate, my Everything! All of a sudden the complaints that caused me such lifelong hopelessness that nearly grieved me to the point of suicide seems so petty and insignificant! And to think that I almost ended my life because of that lonely emptiness from being rejected and not feeling loved! At long last my heart is full, my soul is complete!

Heavenly Father knows all my sins and all the secrets of my heart for His Holy Spirit dwells therein. He knows the shame in my heart for taking the love of Jesus and all that He has done for me for granted. I truly do repent, and I know I am forgiven. I have been cleansed by the Redeeming Blood of Jesus Christ. Jesus truly is my Everything and I shall never forget that! My love for Him comes from deep within my very soul! I wish to proclaim to the whole world… ***"I love You Jesus, with all that I am!"***

> *"Repent therefore and be converted, that your sins may be blotted out, so that times of refreshing may come from the presence of the Lord,"* <u>Acts 3:19</u> (NKJV)

GOD has been longsuffering (patient) with me while the milk of babes was sinking into my heart, eradicating the foolishness within and preparing me for the meat of His Word. I keep telling you, ignorance is no excuse. Everything you need to know about everything that has ever existed, does exist, and ever will exist can be found in the pages of <u>The HOLY BIBLE</u>. All one has to do is read and study it. All one has to do to have 24/7 access to Father GOD is to grab tightly hold of Jesus' right hand, keep His love in your heart and never let Him go.

Can you visualize Jesus standing there before you? He is you know! He is waiting for you to ask Him into your heart and accept His life changing love. He is right there with you, weeping, knocking at the door to your heart and waiting with outstretched arms. Jesus loves you! He loves you! I implore you; do not take His love for granted as I did for so long. And do not throw His love away! It does not matter what your sins are, Jesus loves you just as you are… unconditionally. If you have never invited Jesus into your heart, you can do that right now, right where you are... *no strings attached!*

Open your heart and invite Him in and pray: "Heavenly Father, I believe Jesus is Your only Begotten Son and that He died on the Cross to pay my sin debt. I ask You to forgive me of my sins and I ask Jesus to come into my heart to be my LORD and Savior. Amen"

Your life will change forever. You will have everlasting life with Jesus, your Savior. Nurture your dry bones with His Living Water (read the bible), find a home Church for fellowship and support to help you withstand the fiery darts of the evil schemes of the devil. We need to band together for strength and support in GOD's Word. Let them know you are just a babe in the word of GOD. Do not be embarrassed as we have all had to start somewhere. If you are not accepted, you are in the wrong church.

Remember, it is not about a denomination or a religion; it is about a one-on-one relationship with Jesus Christ, the one and only Son of GOD! Find a church that is filled with the Holy Spirit and the love of Jesus! Talk to Jesus daily as your Friend, your Beloved, as well as your GOD. Seek Him in reverent prayer for He is the LORD thy GOD. Never ever forget to praise and worship Him; giving Him thanks and all the glory for all things in your life; good or bad.

"In everything give thanks: for this is the will of GOD in CHRIST JESUS concerning you." 1 Thessalonians 1:18 (KJV)

Jesus will dispel the darkness that tries to creep into your soul. It is very hard to be depressed when walking, talking and praising in fellowship with Jesus... personally. He is but a breath away and you need never to be lonely again. His love will blow you away!

"Rejoice evermore." 1 Thessalonians 1:16 (KJV)

Yes, I shall rejoice evermore, basking in His protection, strength and love. Loving Jesus is the easiest thing I have ever done in my entire life. What He started within me after my moment of surrender (my Damascus moment) has come full circle! My eyes have been opened as to why I surrendered to Him in the first place!

> *"If the SON therefore shall make you free, ye shall be free indeed." John 8:36 (KJV)*
>
> *"Jesus answered: 'Don't you know me, Phillip, even after I have been among you such a long time?'" John 14:9 (NIV)*

Yes Jesus! I know you now! I know that as great as my compassion and love is for You, Your agape, Your passion for me is greater; immeasurable, incomprehensible and indecipherable. At last I am free of the depression, loneliness and self-pity that I suffered for what seems like all my life! I now can "hear" the love You have for me in the voice of Your written Word! I can "see" Your love in everything around me and all that You have done for me! It is not about me and my brokenness at all; it is about what I have done to You, Jesus, and the brokenness You suffered for me!

I have made You too familiar and I have taken You for granted! I am truly mortified to the very marrow of my bones! This has truly been another miraculous day! Thus far, the journey of writing this book has been exhilarating, enlightening and freeing! I am FREE from forty-years of bondage! Chains have been broken!

Thank you, Jesus, for loving me so much that you gave your all to give me all. Thank you, Sweet Jesus, Whom my soul loves, for opening my heart and my ears that I may feel Your Breath, Your Word, and hear Your Sweet Voice in my heart and in my very soul. I shall never forget the words You wrote upon my heart today:

'I Am He that stands before you daily...
I Am He that loves you unconditionally and for evermore...
There Is No Other!'

Jesus is Agape!
Nanette Crapo April 10, 2019

> *"Place me like a seal over your heart, like a seal on your arm; for love is as strong as death, its jealousy unyielding as the grave, it burns like blazing fire, like a mighty flame."* **SONG OF SOLOMON 8:6** (NIV)

❀ ❀ ❀

"And being found in appearance as a man, He humbled Himself and became obedient to the point of death, even the death of the cross." Philippians 2:8 (NKJV)

❀ ❀ ❀

CHAPTER 3

The Cross
Passion In Action

◦ ◦ ◦

"The only thing that counts is faith expressing itself through love." <u>Galatians 5:6</u> (NIV)

I knew Jesus died on the Cross for my sins, but I am just now understanding the concept behind the Cross and the sheer magnitude of the torture and the anguish that Jesus suffered for me there. I had never thought about how unbearable His pain must have been; or that He might still remember that agony every time He relives it with us when we are suffering. I am only now understanding that Jesus had to bear the Cross for us in order to break the bondage of the curse of the law of sin and death which was upon all of us from generations past. Any other kind of death would not have satisfied the payment...

"Christ has redeemed us from the curse of the law, having become a curse for us, (for it is written, Cursed is everyone who hangs on a tree,") <u>Galatians 3:13</u> (NKJV)

The wooden Cross *(a tree) fulfilled* prophesy that crushed our curses! *Jesus was and is the spotless, sinless Lamb of GOD. Only Jesus's Blood was Worthy, as our Sacrificial Lamb, to cleanse us and pay our sin debt. Jesus knew if He did not follow through... the whole world would be lost and without hope. It was all so very carefully orchestrated by Father GOD in His glorious plan of salvation!*

I can visualize that the Cross He bore upon His back was my sins which in effect was me! He took all the sins and curses of the world into or upon himself to become a substitute for us on that Cross; defeating death, hell, and the grave with His own Life. That was the ***only way*** to pay the penalty of sin, which was and is death. Jesus' faith in, and Agape for, Father GOD gave Him the strength to obey the will of Father GOD. That faith and passion was demonstrated when He carried our Cross. No greater love exists than the Passion, the Agape that our Savior, Jesus Christ, has for Father GOD which He extends to you, to me, and to the whole world!

Would you deny Him your love after all He has done for you and all He has suffered for you? I pray that you do not deny Him. I pray you open your heart to Him!

REMEMBER:

Jesus was on death row for crimes He was not guilty of.

- Jesus knew the suffering that He faced.
- Jesus had the power to stop the crucifixion at any time.
- *Jesus obeyed Father GOD's will out of Faith that Father GOD would keep His Promise and raise Him from the grave on the third day! AGAIN... WOW!*

ANOTHER REVELATION! Jesus obeyed Father GOD in Faith! Jesus trusted Father GOD with His Life when He was here as man, born of a woman! How many times have I read that? I just now understand how much faith in Father GOD it took for Jesus to take my place in death! Faith in Father GOD's promises, faith in things that had never been done before! Jesus was the first to trust by faith that He would be resurrected by the Spirit of Life, the Spirit of GOD! He suffered death and was quickened (made alive) just as promised. Jesus is telling us to trust in Him and believe! He is not asking us to do anything that He has not already done, and His last words were, **"*It Is Finished!*"** (John 19:30)

> *"... looking unto Jesus, the author and finisher of our faith, who for the joy that was set before Him endured the cross, despising the shame, and has sat down at the right hand of the throne of GOD."* <u>Hebrews 12:2</u> (NKJV)

Jesus could not be stoned, thrown off a cliff or killed while here as man until it was His appointed time to die on the Cross for us sinners. He had the power to escape at any time.

> *"Then they took up stones to throw at Him; but Jesus hid Himself and went out of the temple, going through the midst of them, and so passed by."* <u>John 8:59</u> (NKJV)

Then when the soldiers came to arrest Him, He surrendered Himself to them as part of GOD's plan of salvation. He could have stopped everything with just a word.

> *"'Or do you think that I cannot now pray to My Father, and He will provide Me with more than twelve legions of angels? How then could the Scriptures be fulfilled, that it must happen thus?'"* <u>Matthew 26:53-54</u> (NKJV)

> *"So Jesus said to Peter, 'Put your sword into the sheath. Shall I not drink the cup which My Father has given Me?'"* <u>John 18:11</u> (NKJV)

Awesome! That adds even more intensity to my faith in the things that I cannot see! I now have an insight into this mystery of mysteries! Maybe you already knew such things, but I am just now seeing it with eyes of understanding!

This news is indeed "good news" and very elating to my soul! GOD did it for Jesus and has promised to do the same for me! And you have His promise as well, if you ask forgiveness of your sins and accept Jesus, the Only Begotten Son of GOD, as your Savior! Trust and belief through faith in Jesus is the only way to receive the gift of His Holy Spirit; the self-same Spirit that ensures us everlasting life!

> *"And if Christ is in you, the body is dead because of sin, but the Spirit of Him who raised Jesus from the dead dwells in you. He who raised Christ from the dead will also give life to your mortal bodies through His Spirit who dwells in you."* <u>Romans 8:10-11</u> *(NKJV)*

Jesus had to be "dead" in order to be "raised from the dead"! His Spirit did not instantly take Him to Heaven to be with Father GOD. He descended into hell to pay our debt *in full* so that we (believers in Jesus Christ) do not have to go there at all!

Some people I have talked to do not believe that Jesus went into hell at all. Is there some other way to pay the debt of sin which is "death" without dying and going to hell? If so, where was Jesus and what was He doing for those three days? And why was the crucifixion of Jesus necessary? Those are questions I offer for your consideration. As for me, I believe it was and is and always will be as Jesus demonstrated through His agape.

I have always believed in my heart that Jesus gave His life for me because He loves me, but there is so much more involved here as I have discovered in the pages of <u>The Holy Bible</u>. The law had to be upheld. GOD could not break His own laws and let us go into heaven without our sin debt being paid in full. If He could have, there would not have been a need for the crucifixion of Jesus in the first place! Our sins had to be paid for with our lives, thus we were all bound for hell eternal! Jesus went in our place and freed us from the law of sin and death!

Jesus could not just die and go into hell with the Spirit of Life within Himself! So how does one take "life", the eternal life of the Holy Spirit, and make it "dead"? It would have been impossible! I submit to you that Jesus had to give up that "life", the Holy Spirit, to Father GOD. He did it in faith of the promise of receiving it back again! Think about this… the only way to enter hell with the sins of the world upon Himself was to give up His Holy Spirit into the hands of Father GOD, as found in Matthew, Luke and John!

> ***"And Jesus cried out again with a loud voice and yielded up His spirit." Matthew 27:50*** (NKJV)

*Jesus "**yielded up**" (surrendered) His spirit to GOD.*

> ***"And when Jesus had cried out with a loud voice, He said 'Father, into Your hands I commit My spirit.'" Luke 23:46*** (NKJV)

Jesus "***committed***" (*entrusted*) His spirit into the hands of Father GOD.

> ***"When Jesus therefore had received the vinegar, he said, 'It is finished: and he bowed his head, and gave up the ghost." John 19:30*** (KJV)

Jesus "gave up" (sacrificed) His Spirit to God.

It very much sounds to me like Jesus literally surrendered His Spirit over to Father GOD in faith, separating Himself completely from Father GOD, and trusting Father GOD to return His Spirit back to Him. **Father GOD then returned the Spirit of Life back to Jesus to**

resurrect Him from death, hell and the grave! And the devil did not see it coming! Praise GOD!

Jesus was dead, as in the slain Lamb of GOD, which satisfied the payment for our sins. How could Jesus receive *"the promise of the Spirit through faith"* (Galatians 3:14) and be quickened if He did not first give that spirit up?

The same Spirit that brought Jesus back from the grave is promised to us through faith! Because of Jesus, we bypass the dying and the grave part. We are quickened and have victory over death itself because Jesus did that part for us! Praise GOD! Thank you Jesus!

> *"I am He who lives, and was dead, and behold, I am alive forevermore!"* **Revelation 1:18** *(NKJV)*

> *"Verily, verily, I say unto you, if a man keep my saying, he shall never see death."* **John 8:51** (KJV)

I contend that during this temporary period of time that Jesus was in hell He was truly without the Spirit of Life, completely separated from Father GOD. Is it any wonder that He was anguished to the point of sweating blood?

- Jesus was the Firstborn of GOD, born of woman, made flesh like we are;
- Jesus was the first to be quickened and returned from the grave never to die again!
- Jesus set the example for us: believe by faith and receive the promise of the Spirit of Life!
- Jesus proved GOD's Word to be truth when He indeed arose from the grave defeating death forever because He believed... by faith!
- Jesus trusted and loved His Father with the trusting faith of a child and expressed His faith through the action of His passion at the Cross!

- GOD loved us so much that He sent His only Begotten Son to save all who believe on Him with the trusting faith of a child!
- We must believe through faith the same promises of GOD:
We have a Savior in The Lamb of GOD
Through Him we receive His Holy Spirit
Holy Spirit gives us everlasting life
We bypass death, hell and the grave!

In Jesus we have a Lamb so perfect and so loved by Father GOD that He was sacrificed once. Once was enough to cover all our sins for all of the world for all of eternity!

> *"So, Christ was once offered to bear the sins of many; and unto them that look for Him shall He appear the second time without sin unto salvation." Hebrews 9:28* (KJV)

It is only out of His obedience that Jesus submitted His will to the will of Father GOD and carried our Cross! That was quite a cup to bear!

> *"For just as through the disobedience of the one man the many were made sinners, so also through the obedience of the one man the many will be made righteous." Romans 5:19* (NIV)

(The disobedience of the one man being Adam, and the obedience of the One Man being Jesus!)

When we believe in Jesus and what He did for us at the Cross, we do not have to go where He went... death, hell and the grave!

> *"Simon Peter asked Him, 'LORD, where are you going?' 'Where I am going you cannot follow now, but you will follow later.'" John 13:36* (NIV)

Peter could not follow Jesus "*now*" because Jesus was destined to be crucified and headed to hell in our place! Peter could not follow Jesus in death "*now*" because Jesus had yet to pay our sin debt. Jesus had not yet been crucified fulfilling the promise of the Holy Spirit and everlasting life. Only after Jesus was Crucified could Peter receive the same Holy Spirit that gave Jesus life after He laid His down at the Cross.

What did Jesus do in hell? It is written that He not only paid our sin debt, but He preached to the saints and released souls that had died before His crucifixion.

> *"For Christ also suffered once for sins, the just for the unjust, that He might bring us to God, being put to death in the flesh but made alive by the Spirit by whom also He went and preached to the spirits in prison, who formerly were disobedient, when once the Divine longsuffering waited in the days of Noah, while the ark was being prepared, in which a few, that is eight souls, were saved through water." **1 Peter 3:18-20*** (NKJV)

Only then could any of us follow where Jesus ultimately went... heaven, and see Him seated at the right hand of GOD!

> *"My father's house has many rooms; if it were not so, would I have told you that I am going there to prepare a place for you?" **John 14:2*** *(NIV)*

Praise be to our LORD and Savior, the Lamb of GOD for holding the keys to death and hell so that we cannot (do not have to) follow where He went.

> *"...And I have the keys of Hades and Death." **Revelation 1:18*** *(NKJV)*

But we can follow Him to Father GOD's mansion when He has prepared a place for us. He has promised to give us the keys to heaven…

> *"And I will give you the keys of the kingdom of heaven, and whatever you bind on earth will be bound in heaven, and whatever you loose on earth will be loosed in heaven." Matthew 16:19* (NKJV)

His finished works at the Cross paid the ransom to redeem us. The proof is in the scars that are in the palms of His hands. My name, (Nanette), as well as your name, (Child of GOD), is written in those scars!

> **"See, I have inscribed you on the palms of my hands;" Isaiah 49:16** (NKJV)

Then on the third day, He was resurrected, and Mary Magdalene saw Him.

> *"Jesus said to her, 'Do not cling to Me, for I have not yet ascended to My Father; but go to My brethren and say to them, 'I am ascending to My Father and your Father, and to My God and your God.'" John 20:17* (NKJV)

Jesus said that He had not yet ascended to Father GOD, but in the evening of the same day…

> *"Then, the same day at evening, being the first day of the week, when the doors were shut where the disciples were assembled, for fear of the Jews, Jesus came and stood in the midst, and said to them, 'Peace be with you.'" John 20:19* (NKJV)

Satan does not want you to know that Jesus has already set you free from death and the grave because the fear of death is Satan's only weapon to lead you into his pit of depression. Satan does not want you to know that Jesus has reclaimed authority over him, and furthermore, that Jesus has given that authority to those who believe!

The devil holds the fear of death over nonbelievers keeping them in a state of tears and depression about getting older and dying; however, please remember... the devil is the father of lies, so do no fall for his deceit!

> *"He replied, 'I saw Satan fall like lightning from heaven. I have given you authority to trample on snakes and scorpions and to overcome all the power of the enemy; nothing will harm you.'"* **Luke 10:18-19** (NIV)

Jesus gives us victory over death!

> *"However, do not rejoice that the spirits submit to you, but rejoice that your names are written in heaven."* **Luke 10:20** (NIV)

I thank You Jesus, Yeshua, our Messiah, that Satan cannot control me with the fear of death!

> *"O death, where is thy sting? O grave, where is thy victory?"* **I Corinthians 15:55** (KJV)

> *"So when this corruptible has put on incorruption, and this mortal has put on immortality, then shall be brought to pass the saying that is written, 'Death is swallowed up in victory.'"* **1 Corinthians 15:54** (NKJV)

I praise Jesus for His love and faithfulness!

> *"But God demonstrates His own love toward us, in that while we were still sinners, Christ died for us."*
> *Romans 5:8* (NKJV)

The blinders of ignorance are definitely falling off and I can now "see" and fully appreciate Jesus and all He has done for me!

> *"And this is the will of Him who sent Me, that everyone who sees the Son and believes in Him may have everlasting life; and I will raise him up at the last day."*
> *John 6:40* (NKJV)

I now repeat, *"Jesus is Agape, Jesus is Love."* All that He did was done out of Agape. This then is GOD's promise: everlasting life through belief in His Son, Jesus Christ, who expressed His faith through the action of His passion at the Cross!

Nanette Crapo 01/25/2020

> *"Therefore My Father loves Me, because I lay down my life that I may take it again." John 10:17* (NKJV)

> *"The sting of death is sin, and the strength of sin is the law. But thanks be to GOD, who gives us the victory through our LORD Jesus Christ."*
> *1 Corinthians 15:56-57* (NKJV)

Section 5
Saving Souls

○ ○ ○

"No one can come to Me unless *the Father who sent Me draws him, and I will raise him up at the last day.*"
<u>*John 6:44*</u> (KJV)

"*To them God willed to make known what are the riches of the glory of this mystery among the Gentiles; which is Christ in you, the hope of glory.*"
<u>*1 Colossians 1:27*</u> (NKJV)

◦ ◦ ◦

"For the Promise is unto you, and to your children, and to all who are afar off, even as many as the LORD our GOD shall call." Acts 2:39 (KJV)

◦ ◦ ◦

Chapter 1
Ekklesia
Called By My Soul's Mate

● ● ●

"ABBA, ABBA, BABA EKKLESIA!"
Nanette Crapo, 1994

These words were spoken through tears of joy over and over and over again all the way back to my seat when I was baptized in the Holy Spirit in 1994. It would be almost 25 years later before I knew that I was actually speaking "in tongues", in another language, (Greek). Let me clarify, the Holy Spirit was speaking on my behalf to Father GOD saying:

"*Father, Father, baby set apart*" (set apart or called to serve Jesus)... **profound! His Word is alive and lives within me!**

> "*And because you are sons, God has sent forth the Spirit of His Son into your hearts, crying out, 'Abba, Father.'*"
> <u>Galatians 4:6</u> *(NKJV)*

At that time, I definitely was just a baby in GOD's kingdom, feeding on the milk of His Holy Word. Truth be known, I still am, but I learn more and more daily. The more I learn, the more I seek to learn.

During Bible study in 2017, I learned that the above words that I spoke are Greek. Also, I learned during that Bible study that the word ekklesia is used to describe the body of the church. During bible study we learned that the early church was actually a gathering of people as there were no church buildings in the days of Jesus. Most gatherings of Christians were in homes. Ekklesia referred to the gathering of those people that were gathered together to serve Jesus.

Remembering when I spoke those words still leaves me in awe and wonder! I had a personal experience with Jesus Christ through Holy Spirit and did not fully understand it at the time! Wow! Can you imagine my excitement when I heard the word "ekklesia" that day in Bible study? That word had been burned into my memory and into my heart even though I did not know what I had said.

I thought I was saying something about love when I said, "Abba, Abba" as I felt such an overwhelming sense of love that it brought me to tears of joy! Guess what? Abba is Daddy in Greek. Daddy as in Father GOD and GOD is love! (1 John 4:8 & 16) I was blown away, especially since I had a burning desire to find out if I had said anything at all or if I was just babbling. Or, if I was speaking with the *tongues of angels* as mentioned by Paul in 1 Corinthians 13:1.

> *"Though I speak with the tongues of men and of angels, but have not love, I have become sounding brass or a clanging cymbal."* <u>*1 Corinthians 13:1*</u> (NKJV)

It is my understanding that the tongues of angels is known and understood only by GOD and not even the devil knows what is being said. It is also my understanding that it is a language of prayer in the Spirit to GOD on your behalf. So, I was trying to understand if I had spoken in that supernatural language of angels or not. But here is the awesome part of this story: My search started just three weeks prior to that bible study where I heard *"ekklesia"*. Another example of how GOD can speak to us through other people and events to answer prayers and questions when we seek.

My search had actually started in an English to French dictionary, but to no avail. I had taken French in high school and "baba ekklesia" sounded a little like "biblioteque". (Well, it did to me, you know, the way it rolls off the tongue as one long word.) So, I thought it might be French. (Oh well, I was trying, but I was wrong.) I find it so very exciting and beyond description that GOD provided me with an answer shortly after I started seeking. Mystery solved; *"Seek and you shall find..."* (*Luke 11:9*)

Holy Spirit that dwells within me was speaking to Abba, Father GOD on my behalf that I was to be set aside to serve Jesus. I spoke in a real language, albeit foreign to me, Greek, but it was not in the language of angels. That revelation still leaves me in awe of His amazing ability to "speak" directly to me and through me! My mind is still trying to wrap itself around that! It reminds me of the night Holy Spirit screamed for me! Story can be found in my book, ANGELS SPIRITS AND A 9 MM SCREW, Legacy Of Faith And Love Through Five Generations.

That GOD has set me aside to have the honor of serving Jesus Christ still sends chills of delight down my spine and brings me to tears. All that GOD does is purposeful; to prepare us for His greater plan. I find that to be just as splendid as discovering what the Holy Spirit said, through me, on my behalf!

"For through Him we both have access by one Spirit to the Father." Ephesians 2:18 (NKJV)

I do not boast as though He only calls a select few, for I know better. I am humbled and honored that He should still want me after calling me over 25 years ago. That in itself just goes to show you that He truly is longsuffering. He does not give up on us. Praise GOD for that!

It was His calling for me to be a nurse or I would have not excelled beyond my own abilities. All the glory to GOD! And it is His calling in this season of my life to write the books that He has anointed and placed in my heart to write. I have already mentioned that I am nothing without Him and without Him there would be nothing to write! Without Jesus, I would not have a reason for existing. He has purchased me with His blood. He has saved me with His agape. His Holy Spirit is within me.

Anyone can be baptized in the Holy Spirit as long as they have accepted Jesus as their Savior. It is not about religion at all; ***it is all*** *about a personal one-on-one relationship with Jesus Christ, the Son of GOD.* I still marvel at the supernatural ways of GOD; the mystery of His ways! I cannot get enough of His Living Waters and His Bread of Life, which is Jesus Christ!

To worship Jesus and spread the gospel among the heathen is kind of hard to do when I myself was such a stubborn and self-righteous heathen ignorant of GOD's Word. Holy Spirit has done much work within. He is preparing me to serve Jesus as part of the body of the Church.

> *"But when it pleased GOD, who separated me from my mother's womb, and called me by His grace, to reveal His Son in me, that I might preach Him among the heathen..."* <u>Galatians 1:15-16</u> (KJV)

> *"And don't grieve GOD's Holy Spirit. You were sealed by Him for the day of redemption."* <u>Ephesians 4:30</u> (KJV)

I know I grieved Holy Spirit sorely during those forty years of disobedience. I have publicly repented and rededicated my life to serving my LORD and Savior, Jesus Christ. This occurred at **New Vision Baptist Church** in Halls, Tennessee, October of 2018 after **Pastor Mark Rager's** sermon reminded me of GOD's forgiveness of all our sins, even those secret one's that only you and GOD know about. You know, the ones that shame you to your very core. And that we are to forgive ourselves and others that have hurt us; without judging. He reminded me that we are all sinners, otherwise we would not need Jesus.

It was during that sermon that I was able to visibly see the personal relationship Pastor Mark Rager has with Jesus. He was encouraging everyone to seek GOD and experience our own personal encounter. His message was the spark that lit the fire of my desire to be closer to Jesus, to hear His voice daily (down deep inside) as I heard it when He said, "Read Psalms". I have subconsciously been longing to hear Jesus daily; to have that personal relationship that **Pastor Mark** was talking about.

This book, this current journey, is building that relationship. Each verse, each word enlightens me and draws me nearer and nearer to Him. This journey with Jesus is a marvelous, mysterious, and life altering experience! It is an intense journey of learning through Scripture of the mysteries of Jesus Christ. This journey is healing for my soul.

It was very liberating to publicly cleanse my soul. I am thankful to my childhood friend, **Janet Chalk Peyton Sanders**, for taking me to her Church while vacationing with her and her family, thus giving me the opportunity to hear **Pastor Mark Rager**. Although she remarried after being widowed and moved far, far away, our relationship of "sisterhood" remains as it was in grade school. Through her I was led to that sermon on that day and it was just what GOD knew I needed to hear and witness for myself. Again, this is an excellent example of what I have touched on again and again: GOD can "speak" to us through visions, dreams... and other people.

Once Jesus calls you (*ekklesia*) to serve Him, you become part of His Church, His bride and He becomes your Bridegroom. Jesus is the Bridegroom of His Church. GOD has included gentiles (non-Jews) to share in the promise of the inheritance of His Kingdom through His Only Begotten Son Jesus Christ. Hallelujah! Praise GOD for Jesus!

> *"The Spirit Himself bears witness with our spirit that we are children of God, and if children, then heirs—heirs of God and joint heirs with Christ, if indeed we suffer with Him, that we may also be glorified together."*
> <u>**Romans 8:16-17**</u> (NKJV)

We have all suffered as evident in our scars. Ekklesia... GOD is calling upon us to go forth and be a witness to the Gospel of Jesus Christ. He is calling upon us to give our testimonials of the treachery and deceit we have suffered at the hands of Satan, of the lovingkindness of GOD, of the forgiveness of our sins through Jesus Christ, and of the gift of eternal life. Our *good works* is to share Jesus and His love with the whole world!

> *"For we are God's workmanship, created in Christ Jesus to do good works, which God prepared in advance for us to do."* <u>Ephesians 2:10</u> (NIV)

Let those that have ears and eyes take heed of GOD's Word for it is written and GOD's Word is Truth. GOD cannot lie. Jesus is coming again for His bride, His Church, His ekklesia. I pray you answer and are ready when He returns.

> *"And at midnight a cry was heard: 'Behold, the bridegroom is coming; go out to meet Him!'"* <u>Matthew 25:6</u> (NKJV)

> *"...The Bridegroom came; and they that were ready went in with Him to the marriage: and the door was shut."* <u>Matthew 25:10</u> (KJV)

Once Jesus returns the door will be shut and it will be too late to choose to be with Him forever! You must choose *before* He returns!

> *"...'LORD, LORD, open to us!' But He answered and said, 'Assuredly, I say to you, I do not know you.'"* <u>Matthew 25:11-12</u> (NKJV)

The above last words I shall never hear thanks to Jesus. For I am a child of Abba, Father GOD, adopted through the Blood of Jesus Christ... are you?

GOD draws us to believe on the name of His Only Begotten Son, Jesus Christ for the promise of everlasting life. He draws everyone with love. Sadly, some will resist! As Christians we are to spread the gospel (good news) of Jesus Christ. If anyone rejects Him then their fate is on them. One cannot force another person to answer GOD's calling any more than one can answer another's calling for them. I know because I tried. It just does not work that way. The decision must be of one's own free will, which has been given to everyone by our Creator, Father GOD.

> *"There is one body, and one Spirit, even as ye are called in one hope of your calling; One Lord, one faith, one baptism, One God and Father of all, who is above all, and through all, and in you all." Ephesians 4:4-6* (KJV)

> *"But now in Christ Jesus you who once were far away have been brought near through the Blood of Christ." Ephesians 2:13* (NIV)

◦ ◦ ◦

"Put on the full armor of GOD so that you can take your stand against the devil's schemes. For our struggle is not against flesh and blood, but against the rulers, against the authorities, against the powers of this dark world and against the spiritual forces of evil in the heavenly realms." Ephesians 6:11-12 (NIV)

◦ ◦ ◦

Chapter 2

Armor Of God

○ ○ ○

It is not only necessary to know GOD's Word for life's important decisions, but it is essential to know how to protect oneself against the evil schemes of Satan. Most of us have no idea that the devil attacks us daily! Some people do not believe in GOD because they are brainwashed by television that ancient aliens have been mistaken for gods and therefore GOD is not real. However, these same people believe in and search out the paranormal evil entities, ghost hauntings and so on that they have also seen on television. How can one believe in the evil (Satan) supernatural world and not the marvelous Sovereign Goodness (GOD) of the supernatural world?

I say "Wake Up People! GOD is real and so is the devil and his evil demons!" They are both very, very real. They are both surrounding us daily, battling for our souls. Wake up to the reality of the supernatural for you are in the middle of it! The devil is jealous of the love that GOD lavishes upon us and the worship and love that we lavish upon GOD. Satan wants that worship from us for himself!

When you pray for GOD's guidance and direction, He will answer you through Holy Spirit if you have accepted Jesus as your Lord and Savior. If His Word is in your heart, you will recognize scriptures when

He speaks to you. If what you hear does not line up with His Word in Scripture then it is not from GOD. GOD does not contradict Himself.

We are warned in Deuteronomy and again in Revelation that we are not to add or take away from GOD's Word as it is written. I believe if we do add to or take away from the truth as it was written, then it could become distorted. Satan is an expert at distorting GOD's Word to trick us into believing we are doing what GOD's Word says to do. When the enemy (the devil) manipulates GOD's Word, he makes it sound good and right when in truth, it is against Scripture. This point, in part, is the essence of my testimony. I allowed myself to be wronged because of wrong believing in the distorted words of the deceiver because of my ignorance of GOD's Truth.

> *"For I testify unto every man that heareth the words of the prophecy of this book, If any man shall add unto these things, GOD shall add unto him the plagues that are written in this book: And if any man shall take away from the words of the book of this prophecy, GOD shall take away his part out of the book of life, and out of the holy city, and from the things which are written in this book."* <u>Revelation 22:18-19</u> (KJV)

That sounds pretty severe to me! I am being very careful to copy word for word in each Scripture that I use; especially those in the book of Revelation!

The danger in changing GOD's Word is that it can become unrecognizable. It can become someone's interpretation of what they think GOD was saying instead of a true translation. One must be careful. I myself have found a discrepancy between the KJV and another well-known Bible which I shall not name. Let me just tell you the discrepancy I found.

KJV (King James Version) says we are to forgive 70 X 7 times, which is 490 times. Another Bible I referenced says we are to forgive seventy-seven times! Big difference. I can count 77 times as I forgive the same person over and over. The point is we are not keep count, not keep track. The point is to forgive as many times as necessary... # lost in translation!

If one does not recognize GOD's Word because of severe alterations, then the devil will swoop in and twist it even further to manipulate one into believing his lies. Do not be fooled by Satan's lies. His promises are things of this world, things that do not last, things that do not matter in death, things that one can neither take to heaven nor to hell. Then when one has been completely broken, one will be discarded, thrown away into the deep dark abyss of eternal misery and darkness.

Are you in danger of losing your eternal soul? Your eternity could be in eternal darkness! GOD forbid this from happening to you, your loved ones or even your enemies! You may not believe in such things, but... what if you are wrong? Arm yourself with GOD's Word. And please remember that Satan is incapable of promising you anything, because he is not capable of telling the truth! On the other hand, GOD's promises are truth because He is not capable of telling a lie! GOD's written Word is His Spoken Living Word... it was not to be altered! Accurately translated but not altered.

I would like to add, please do not mistake GOD or Satan for aliens as the television tries to make you believe! I am not saying aliens do not exist. But I know in faith that if they do, GOD is GOD over them too! Evil spirits do not require a spaceship and neither do GOD's angels! Remember the dark shadowy entities that I have witnessed as seeing swirling around in that hospital room! I can testify that there were no spaceships involved and no light beams! There was only darkness!

Although Satan is also supernatural, he is not omnipresent as is GOD Almighty. The devil cannot be in more than one place at one time. Only GOD can be everywhere at the same time. The devil uses demons, evil spirits, minions, dark entities and such to trap people in his pits and snares. Dark evil spirits that dwell inside many poor souls here on earth, manipulating them into doing his evil bidding. Of this I also have first-hand knowledge as a witness thereof. I wrote in my first book about some of the evil manifestations I have seen with my own eyes.

My spiritual eyes and ears had been closed in my disobedience until I surrendered my will and cried out to Jesus for help. His immediate response was mind blowing to me! That was the first time that I had a very personal encounter with Jesus! My very first one-on-one with My Savior! I have not been the same since that day! I have been preparing myself for this supernatural war with knowledge through understanding of His Words of wisdom. I already had the helmet of salvation through Jesus Christ and now I have taken the sword of the Spirit!
Nanette Crapo 2/2020

> ***"Take the helmet of salvation and the sword of the Spirit, which is the word of GOD." Ephesians 6:17*** (NIV)

There are supernatural weapons that GOD has provided for those of you that seek and accept Him as Truth. I have discussed in my first book the existence of GOD's angels that we cannot see. They surround us in this supernatural spiritual warfare without tangible means of transportation (spaceships) or tangible weapons. I now want to explore the full armour of GOD with you, found in Ephesians. This is the only armour that is effective against the dark spiritual forces that come against us daily. GOD would not have us go out among the wolves without the protection of His armour, His Word...

> ***"I am sending you out like sheep among wolves. Therefore, be as shrewd as snakes and as innocent as doves." Matthew 10:16*** (NIV)

I was talking with my dearly beloved lifelong (since fifth grade) childhood friend and sister in Christ, **Janet Chalk Payton Sanders** about GOD's protection on a recent visit with her and her family. She has remarried since being widowed and moved to another state, but that does not keep us apart. It is extremely important for me to have friends that share my passion for Christ. During that visit she and I had some quality devotional time along with her biological sisters, and my sisters in Christ, whom I also love, **Kathy Chalk Richardson** and **Miss Tina Chalk**. During one such devotional, we discussed this *full armour of GOD* which is found in Ephesians 6:10-19.

My point being that even going to church once or twice a week does not give one the depth and insight into GOD's Word that one needs for protection and survival against the daily onslaught of evil forces that come against us. One must, and I stress... *must*, spend time daily in prayer, in worship, and in fellowship with our brothers and sisters in Christ.

We are all children of Abba, Father GOD. We are family. We four agreed on all of these points. We gained much new insight, understanding and knowledge during our devotional times that would have taken several months or even years of a once-a-week church service. Knowledge of the gospel of Jesus is not only a game changer, but a life changer! The name of Jesus in Hebrew is *Yeshua*, which means Savior.

So, in addition to attending Sunday school and church services one must study at home or with friends as well. There is just so much valuable information concerning life and death matters that we cannot afford to miss out on any of it! Drawing nearer to GOD should be a lifelong journey of study and discovery. As for me, it will be!

I refuse to continue to dwell upon the forty plus years in which I have missed out on this marvelous relationship with Jesus! The important issue here is that now I do indeed have a relationship with Him! Hallelujah! The more I read and study, the more His mysteries are revealed to me. In turn, the more knowledge of these mysteries I seek. For example, the armour of GOD. Although we remembered hearing *about* it at church, we lacked the depth of understanding of its meaning.

GOD's armour... what a powerful weapon against the devil! I am of the opinion that we need both the full armour of GOD, as well as His supernatural army of angels that He has given charge over us so that we don't strike our foot against a stone. (Psalm 91:12)

> *"For He will command His angels concerning you to guard you in all your ways; they will lift you up in their*

hands, so that you will not strike your foot against a stone." <u>Psalm 91:11-12</u> (NIV)

To have this knowledge is to be armed with the sword of His Truth which is His Word and to have a shield against evil, a shield of faith. Faith comes by reading and hearing His Word. Jesus is the Word. In His Breath is my life. One cannot spread the gospel of Jesus when *ekklesia* (called out or set aside to serve Him) if ignorant of GOD's Word. And one cannot give one's heart fully to Jesus without fully understanding His passion for us and what His passion cost Him! And also, one cannot (or should not) go forth into this evil world without GOD's full armour for protection.

> *"Stand firm then, with the belt of truth buckled around your waist, with the breastplate of righteousness in place, and with your feet fitted with the readiness that comes from the gospel of peace. In addition to all this, take up the shield of faith, with which you can extinguish all the flaming arrows of the evil one. Take the helmet of salvation and the sword of the Spirit, which is the word of GOD." <u>Ephesians 6:14-17</u>* (NIV)

It is up to all believers in Jesus Christ to pray for guidance and wisdom as to what He would have us do; what His calling for us is. All believers should uplift and pray for one another. When we accept Jesus as our Savior, we belong to Him. We should strive to be healthy so we can better serve Him. (Note: I struggled to quit smoking for over three years. When I finally took my addiction to GOD in prayer, I was able to quit literally overnight! I have not stressed the importance of prayer in either book, but prayer is the key to everything once one receives Christ into one's heart.)

> *"Do you not know that your body is a temple of the Holy Spirit, who is in you, whom you have received*

from GOD? You are not your own, you were bought at a price. Therefore, honor GOD with your body."
1 Corinthians 6:19-20 (NIV)

We must arm ourselves with GOD's Word, trust in Jesus and surround ourselves with brothers and sisters in Christ. I thank GOD for his longsuffering with me, for pealing the blinders off my eyes, for pulling my head out of the sand, and for protecting my heart from hardening! The armour of GOD gives us the only powerful weapon of choice to repel the attacks of the enemy, *the flaming arrows of the evil one!* Hallelujah! And make no mistake, Satan is the evil one, the enemy!

To choose the weapon of choice (GOD's armour) is to choose Jesus and to hide His Words in your heart! You will find in GOD's arsenal of weapons the greatest weapon of all... the awesomely powerful name of Jesus (Yeshua)! The Name above all names is Jesus (Yeshua)! I thank GOD for setting my feet upon the Rock... the Foundation of His Word; His Living Word. Jesus is the Cornerstone of the Church, the Foundation, the Rock. There is no other!

Jesus Is My Rock!

"I will show you what he is like who comes to Me and hears My words and puts them into practice. He is like a man building a house, who dug down deep and laid the foundation on rock. When a flood came, the torrent struck that house but could not shake it because it was well built" Luke 6:47-49 (NIV)

❦ ❦ ❦

"You did not choose me, but I chose you, and appointed you so that you might go and bear fruit – fruit that will last – and so that whatever you ask in my name the Father will give you. This is my command, Love each other." John 15:16-17 (NIV)

❦ ❦ ❦

Chapter 3

Mission Of Agape "Follow Me" Mark 8:34

○ ○ ○

"For we are God's workmanship, created in Christ Jesus to do good works, which God prepared in advance for us to do." Ephesians 2:10 (NIV)

Agape is Greek for love, but not just an ordinary kind of love. It is the deep unchangeable, indisputable and incontrovertible love that is expressed through actions without words. That is the kind of love Jesus has for us. Jesus commands that we love one another as He loves us. GOD has chosen me because He loves me. He loves you and is calling you too, but perhaps you are not listening.

It is my prayer that this book "His" book, will bear fruit that will last forever… once published. It is the fruition of the seeds that my grandfather planted in me as a child of 3 ½ years of age when he told me Jesus loves me and wants me to be good, because He cries when I am bad.

GOD made us to be the Church, ekklesia, called, set apart, sanctified to serve Jesus. Jesus is the Bridegroom of the Church, GOD called us out to be the brides of Christ in the body of His Church. We are to love Jesus as our Bridegroom. We are to love one another as Jesus loves us. That is the unconditional, giving, compassionate agape Jesus kind of love. The hearts of believers are flooded with that kind of love through the fruit of the Spirit (Galatians Chapter 5) once we accept Jesus as our LORD and Savior.

Jesus asked Peter three times if he loved Him:

> *"The third time He said to him, 'Simon son of John, do you love me?' Peter was hurt because Jesus asked him the third time, 'Do you love me?' He said, 'Lord, you know all things; you know that I love you.' Jesus said, 'Feed my sheep.' John 21:17* (NIV)

GOD has spoken to me through the scriptures and through this book about not only how to move forward past the fear and pain in my past, but how to plant the seeds to a lost and dying world. He has told me to "write a book" and through it I would "feed" His lost sheep by spreading the gospel of **agape**, the **love Jesus has for all of us.**

> *"The Sovereign LORD has given me a well-instructed tongue, to know the word that sustains the weary. He wakens me morning by morning, wakens my ear to listen like one being instructed." Isaiah 50:4* (NIV)

Agape, Jesus, Yeshua! You have called me to feed your sheep with your Word. I hear you and I submit my will to Your will. Guide me. Guard my thoughts and my words that the truth of Your Holy Word may be heard. For You are worthy O Lamb of GOD, Lion of the tribe of Juda, Bread of Life, Living Waters, my LORD and Savior! Mighty and Powerful is Your precious name, Jesus, Yeshua! I will praise You and love You all the days of my life! I love You, Abba, Father GOD! I love You, Jesus, Yeshua! I want to share Your agape with the world.

Nanette Crapo 01/24/2020

Each of us are different and unique with different talents. Each of us have been given *gifts* according to GOD's will, i.e.: preacher, teacher, worship leader (musically gifted), business, healing (doctor or nurse) etc. They are called *gifts of the Spirit,* in 1 Corinthians 12:8-10, and Romans 12:6-8. They are different than the *fruit of the Spirit*. I have discussed these gifts in length in <u>ANGELS, SPIRITS And A 9 mm SCREW, Legacy Of Faith And Love Through Five Generations</u>. To write the above verses down would cover a full page so I will ask you, the reader, to look them up this time. Just know that some people have more than one gift. It is up to us to seek GOD as to what our gifts are and how we are to use them for His greater purpose and glory. This can only be done by drawing near to Him and having a personal relationship with Jesus, our LORD and Savior. It is from GOD through Holy Spirit that these gifts are given.

> *"But each man has his own gift from God; one has this gift, another has that."* <u>*1 Corinthians 7:7*</u> (NIV)

After my retirement I felt useless, worthless. I asked GOD what He would have me do now to serve Jesus and He led me to writing books. That was the absolute last thing on my mind. That was a little over a year ago and this is my second book. These books are not just books; they are GOD's way to minister to broken and wounded souls with love and compassion through my testimony. I also stay with friends and relatives that are in the hospital, to lift them up in love and with faith in the power of prayer. If I am unable to go to them due to the distance, I still lift them up in prayer. I have strong faith in the healing stripes of Jesus and have witnessed many miraculous healings; some long distance. So, pray for people, pray if you can do nothing else... pray.

> *"For we are His workmanship, created in Christ Jesus for good works, which God prepared beforehand that we should walk in them."* <u>*Ephesians 2:10*</u> (NKJV)

Jesus taught agape; He walked the walk of His agape. He gave His agape to us and for us. Jesus literally gave His all for us to pay our sin debt and give us righteousness through His righteousness.

> *"For GOD so loved the world, that He gave His only Begotten Son, that whosoever should believeth in Him should not perish, but have everlasting life."*
> **John 3:16** (KJV)

Jesus' faith in Father GOD's promise to resurrect Him from the dead on the 3rd day was expressed at the Cross that He carried for us! Faith that Jesus died for our sins, expresses itself through our acceptance of Him as our Savior! My calling is to share my faith (a gift of the Spirit as well as one of the fruits of the Spirit) and my love (a fruit of the Spirit) to touch hurting hearts and shattered souls with sympathy and empathy from the depts of my compassionate heart. And to share the mystery of the gospel that Jesus Christ loves you. He knows and understands everything about you, and yet, He still loves you.

I pray you understand and never forget that Jesus' love for you is strong as death and greater than the burden of the Cross He carried. As Christians we are to show our faith in the finished works of Jesus Christ by spreading the gospel of His agape love. As the beloved children of GOD and joint heirs with Jesus Christ to the kingdom of heaven, we are to demonstrate our faith in His Promise of everlasting life through our actions of kindness and compassion. This is agape. Our mission is a mission of agape, a mission of the love of Jesus Christ. *Jesus is Agape... passion in action as He carried our Cross!*

Agape,
Nanette Crapo
02/25/2020

> *"And that repentance and remission of sins should be preached in His name among all nations..."*
> **Luke 24:47** (KJV)

> *"When He had called the people to Himself, with His disciples also, He said to them, 'Whoever desires to come after me, let him deny himself, and take up his cross, and follow Me.'"* <u>Mark 8:34</u> (NKJV)

If you would like to pick up your cross and follow Jesus, all you have to do is ask forgiveness of your sins and invite Him into your heart to be your LORD and Savior. If you would like to do that, I have included a prayer of salvation that you can recite right now...

Prayer Of Salvation

Heavenly Father, I ask that you forgive me of my sins.

I believe that Jesus Christ is the Son of the Living GOD and that He was crucified in my place, paying my sin debt and freeing me from the curse of the law of sin and death.

I invite You, Jesus, into my heart right now to be my LORD and Savior.

I believe that all my sins have now been forgiven through the power of Your Blood which purchased me and cleansed me of my sins.

In Jesus precious name I pray.

Amen

◦ ◦ ◦

"As the Father loved Me, I also have loved you; abide in My love." John 15:9 (NKJV)

◦ ◦ ◦

Epilogue

○ ○ ○

I pray that your *spiritual* eyes have been opened, as have mine, to the truth of Jesus and His Love for us. He tried to tell me on April 10, 2019 with what I called the "Love Letter". I thought that was deep! His love for us is beyond deep, it is limitless and timeless!

As I have exposed in this book, my ignorance of His Word was shameful and extensive. The original subtitle of this book **AGAPE:** *<u>Love Gave Him Strength to Carry My Cross</u>*, was as far as my depth of knowledge went back in January of 2019, and that was the subtitle that was in my heart. I am now changing that subtitle to <u>**LOVE CARRIED MY CROSS**</u> because:

Jesus *is* **Love**,
Jesus carried my cross; therefore,
Love carried my cross… literally.

For the record, upon completion of this book I have added <u>***Passion In Action***</u> to the cover photo to represent the Heart (the agape love) of Jesus carrying my cross. I now have a profound awareness with a deeper understanding of the meaning of the passion of Christ! His passion is immeasurable! His passion for us comes from the depth of His very Soul! There is no greater love than Jesus Himself and the proof is in His scars! He gave us His capacity to love others through the fruit of the Spirit which is His Holy Spirit that dwells within us. My closing prayer for all…

Thank You Abba, Father GOD, for taking this once broken vessel and putting the pieces of me back together again. You have given me what I have prayed for and so very much more. You have opened my spiritual eyes that I may "see" and better understand the heart of Jesus through Holy Spirit within me. A heart that is overflowing with passion for me and for the whole world. A heart like none other for there is No Other.

All the glory and all the praise for this book belongs to You, Abba, Father GOD, for it is not of me, but Your calling for me, Your will. You have blessed me with a compassionate and loving heart and a strong faith for the Trinity. I worship You, love You and serve You with faith in that which I could not see, touch or smell; but that I can now "see", "hear" and "feel" in my heart.

Thank You Jesus! Thank You for Your Passion, Your Agape Love! I believe by faith that Your every Word is Truth, Light, Love and Life. I know that without You I would not only be lost but I would be nothing... a lost nothingness! Thank You Jesus, Yeshua, for bringing me out of the darkness of depression into Your glorious, radiantly blinding light of love and life. Thank You for calling me, for nurturing me, for protecting me, for loving me and for always being within me! Thank You for expressing Your faith through the strength of Your love; setting the example of what faith is and showing me what true Love Is. You demonstrated that agape when You carried my cross and exchanged Your life for mine, healing my heart, crushing my curses and saving my soul! You are the Agape that is in my heart!

I pray that my testimony will be useful as a witness of GOD's protection, forgiveness, grace, mercy, and love that surpasses time and space. I pray that you turn to Jesus and let Him crush your curses, heal your heart, and save your soul through His great Passion, His Agape.

I pray you, the reader, embrace the love Jesus has for you through a personal relationship with Him and run with it never looking back. If you do, His love will change you forever! You have GOD's Spoken Promises in His written Word: *The Holy Bible*! May GOD Bless You and Your Family. May you hear the call of Jesus in your heart, and answer. May your broken vessel be mended and filled to overflowing with the Love of Jesus Christ, Yeshua, our Messiah, and may you extend that love to others.
With Love In Jesus Name I Pray, Amen.
Nanette Crapo 03/28/2020

I will close with a prayer that my **Grandpa Crapo** said before every meal without fail. It is known as:

The Lord's Prayer

○ ○ ○

"Our Father in heaven,
 Hallowed be Your name.
 Your kingdom come.
 Your will be done
 On earth as it is in heaven.
 Give us this day our daily bread.
 And forgive us our debts,
 As we forgive our debtors.
 And do not lead us into temptation,
 But deliver us from the evil one.
 For Yours is the kingdom and the power and the glory forever.
 Amen."
Matthew 6:9-13 (NKJV)

Addendum

○ ○ ○

COVID 19 PANDEMIC
04/04/2020

"I am the light of the world. He who follows Me shall not walk in darkness, but have the light of life"
<u>John 8:12</u> (NKJV)

As this book comes to completion the COVID-19 virus has become a Pandemic. I have just turned 69 years old and never have I been through something so socially disruptive and economically devastating. The number of sick and dying people world-wide is staggeringly surreal. The stock market is suffering as businesses world-wide are closing and populations of entire major cities are under orders to stay in their homes. Nations have closed their borders, including this great Nation. It truly is of biblical proportions! GOD has touched my heart to add this addendum as **a message of hope!**

"You shall not be afraid of the terror by night,
Nor of the arrow that flies by day,
Nor of the pestilence that walks in darkness,
Nor of the destruction that lays
waste at noonday.
A thousand may fall at your side,
And ten thousand at your right hand;
But is shall not come near you."
<u>Psalm 91:5-7</u> (NKJV)

Maybe, just maybe, you were called *for such a time as this* to give your testimony of how Jesus saved you? Maybe He is calling you to be a witness of His love to the fearful, the lonely, the sick, and the hopeless… who knows?

> *"Yet who knows whether you have come to the kingdom for such a time as this?" **Ester 4:14*** (NKJV)

> *"To give light to those who sit in darkness and the shadow of death, To guide our feet into the way of peace." **Luke 1:79*** (NKJV)

No maybe about it, it is time for us as followers of Jesus Christ to open our mouths and tell the world how He saved us by His grace and love. And it is time to tell the world about GOD's plan of salvation and the gospel of Jesus Christ.

This, then, is my prayer:

We need You, Abba, Father GOD, in this our hour of world-wide devastation! We pray for Your mercy and grace through the mighty name of Your Only Begotten Son, Jesus, to save us from ourselves! I pray that this pandemic resolve suddenly with a breakthrough vaccine or that it break so mysteriously that everyone will know it was the miraculous power of GOD, in the name of Jesus! Amen!

Nanette Crapo 04/04/2020

> *"And the prayer of faith will save the sick, and the Lord will raise him up." **James 5:15*** (NKJV)

> *"Therefore I will look to the LORD; I will wait for the God of my salvation; My GOD will hear me." **Micah 7:7*** (NKJV)

Acknowledgments

To my youngest son, **John Karamitsos**, for your emotional support and encouragement to write this book in truth and honesty about a lifetime of loss born out of traumatic scars of betrayal and rejection. As we have talked, it has become evident that the curse of emotional scars extended beyond self. They extended from my prior generations to my future generations. A curse that only Jesus could break through His demonstration of love for us at the Cross. Thank you, John, for your love and encouragement. In you I see your grandmother's, my mother's, heart; her unconditional Jesus kind of agape love for others. Hold fast and keep the faith!

To both my sons, **John and Tasos Karamitsos**; I thank you for letting me know that you always knew I loved you even though I was "always at work". Though you did not understand my absence at the time, you have both expressed understanding now that you are adults and the main financial provider for your families. You understand being "on call" and "shift work". I love you both more than words can express, and I am equally proud of both of you!

To my nephew, **Steven Chrysafis**, I thank you for your demonstrations of faith and love for Jesus. You have been the inspiration for my thirst for knowledge of GOD's Word. I enjoyed the Bible studies that you shared with me. You opened the windows to the mysteries of Jesus found in The Holy Bible. I distinctly remember you saying that the Light mentioned in The Bible was Jesus. I had never heard that before and it made me thirst to learn more! Mere words cannot express the gratitude that I feel in my heart. Thank you, Steven.

To my sister in Christ who is also my biological sister, **Melinda Sharon Chrysafis;** I extend much appreciation and gratitude for your unwavering love and steadfast encouragement to follow GOD's will to write this book. Without your support and endless hours of proof-reading, this book would not have come to fruition. Thank you, Sister!

To my dear friends and sisters in Christ, **Janet Chalk Payton Sanders and Kathy Chalk Richardson,** who share my passion for Christ, I give my heart felt appreciation for your love, understanding and support. I miss you and I miss our Bible studies.

A very special expression of gratitude and appreciation to my sister in Christ, **Miss Tina Chalk.** In you I recognize the fruit of the Spirit of profound unconditional love, Jesus' agape kind of love, for others. Through you GOD has shown me my heart. Understanding my own heart has helped me better understand *agape*, the love so freely given from the heart of Christ, our Savior. And this has helped me better understand the hearts of those that have betrayed me, that their hearts do not know His love and His love is their only hope.

Thank you, **Miss Tina**, for those private talks where we shared our heart felt pain. Pain that runs so deeply into our souls that no one else we have talked to seems to understand. People that sincerely try to console us with platitudes of "Time heals all wounds", "Just let go" and "Move on". How refreshing and wonderful to find someone that I know really understands, someone that "gets it". Most of all to finally understand that Jesus Himself "gets it" because He has experienced it all.

It is my belief that GOD wants us to use our pain to help others whose hearts have been deeply wounded in the hopes of extending the experience of healing through the love of Jesus Christ. And that His loving heart and healing hands extend to all, even those that have abandoned us. GOD has a purpose for such as ourselves. We are to give our testimonies of the depth of anguish and profound agony our hearts have suffered and how Jesus saved us with His presence and His love... we are not alone. The world is suffering with loneliness and depression. We all need the agape kind of love that can be found only in the arms of Jesus.

Others such as us that have lived through such betrayal and survived the suicidal attempts of depression have a deep understanding of the anguish Jesus suffered for us at the Cross. And yet even we cannot comprehend the totality of His suffering nor of His unconditional and incomprehensible passion for us. We are to share the message of His agape to this world which is so full of darkness. A message as to the truth of His light, love and *life*. A message that we have a Friend that understands, and His mane is Jesus, Yeshua. A message of His agape, His passion for us. A message that Jesus is the only way to Father GOD, our only Savior, and our only true Soul Mate.

*There is **NO OTHER!***

With agape in Christ,
Nanette Crapo
04/04/2020

References

HOLY BIBLE, CONCORDANCE (KJV)
RED LETTER EDITION, King James Version
TRANSLATED OUT OF THE ORIGINAL TONGUES AND WITH THE FORMER TRANSLATIONS DILIGENTLY COMPARED AND REVISED. AUTHORIZED KING JAMES VERSION. THE WORLD PUBLISHING COMPANY.
CLEVELAND AND NEW YORK
PUBLISHED BY THE WORLD PUBLISHING COMPANY 2231 WEST 110TH STREET
CLEVELAND 2 – OHIO
MANUFACTURED IN THE UNITED STATES OF AMERICA

THE HOLY BIBLE, NEW KING JAMES VERSION (NKJV)
Scripture taken from the NEW KING JAMES VERSION. Copyright 1982 by Thomas Nelson. Used by permission. All rights reserved.

THE HOLY BIBLE, NEW INTERNATIONAL VERSION (NIV)
Scripture quotations taken from THE HOLY BIBLE, NEW INTERNATIONAL VERSION, NIV.
Copyright 1973, 1978, 1984, 2011 by Biblica, Inc.
Used by permission. All rights reserved worldwide.
The "NIV" and "New international Version" are trademarks registered in the United States Patent and Trademark Office by Biblica, Inc.

Personal Journals of Nanette Crapo, Author

Special Mention

Sharon Crapo Curry Chrysafis:
Sister, mentor, best friend, and travelling companion. I extend my heartfelt appreciation for your untold hours of proof-reading, your encouragement, and your emotional support. I thank you Sister; more than words can express.
Nanette Crapo

Lightning Source UK Ltd.
Milton Keynes UK
UKHW021823121020
371462UK00005B/164